HAVELOCK

By the same author

R. S. Surtees

Great Men of Durham

MAJOR-GENERAL SIR HENRY HAVELOCK, Bart, K.C.B.

(From the print in the possession of Lady Havelock-Allan)

HAVELOCK

by

Leonard Cooper

THE BODLEY HEAD · LONDON

First published 1957

Made and printed in Great Britain by
WILLIAM CLOWES AND SONS, LIMITED, LONDON AND BECCLES
for THE BODLEY HEAD
10 Earlham Street, London, W.C.2

To

My Wife, Stella Mary,
for our Silver Wedding.

'I will uphold you, trunk and shoot and flowering sheaf
And I will hold you, root and fruit and falling leaf.'

Author's Note

I MUST acknowledge with gratitude the help which I have received from Lady Havelock-Allan and her kindness in lending prints for the illustrations to this book: also the courtesy of the Cresset Press in allowing me to quote the lines from Mrs. E. J. Scovell's poem, 'A Betrothal', in the dedication.

I am, as ever, indebted to Mr. Frank Beckwith, M.A., Librarian of the Leeds Library, whose time and immense erudition have been put so freely at my disposal, and to all the staff of the Library, especially Mr. Bumby and Mr. Walker who have helped so greatly and so pleasantly in my researches. I am glad to add my thanks to Mr. Mark Hamilton of Messrs. A. M. Heath & Co. Ltd. for his help and to Professor Williams of St. Andrews University for valuable criticism and suggestions. I must also express my gratitude to Brigadier J. Clark, O.B.E., for expert advice about India and the Indian Army, and for the loan of books.

Contents

I	THE SAINTS (1795–1823)	*page* 9
II	THE 13TH FOOT (1823)	14
III	THE BURMESE WAR (1824–1826)	17
IV	HANNAH (1826–1838)	24
V	AFGHANISTAN (1838–1840)	32
VI	KABUL (1841)	41
VII	JALALABAD (1841–1842)	50
VIII	THE FORTY-EIGHT HOURS WAR (1842–1843)	62
IX	THE SIKH WAR (1845–1846)	67
X	ENGLAND (1847–1851)	70
XI	THE GREASED CARTRIDGES (1852–1853)	80
XII	QUARTERMASTER-GENERAL (1853–1857)	86
XIII	THE PERSIAN WAR (1857)	93
XIV	MUTINY (1857)	99
XV	ALLAHABAD (1857)	107
XVI	FATEHPUR (1857)	114
XVII	THE MASSACRE AT CAWNPORE (1857)	121
XVIII	CAWNPORE RECAPTURED (1857)	129
XIX	PREPARATION FOR THE RELIEF OF LUCKNOW (1857)	136
XX	'THE OLD GENTLEMAN' (1857)	145
XXI	SUPERSEDED (1857)	152
XXII	ALUM BAGH (1857)	162
XXIII	THE RESIDENCY (1857)	171
XXIV	PIPES AT LUCKNOW (1857)	180
	BOOK LIST	183
	REGIMENTAL NAMES	185
	INDEX	187

CHAPTER I

THE SAINTS (1795–1823)

THE NAME Havelock suggests a Danish origin and attempts have been made, though without success, to trace the family back to that Havlok the Dane, who was the hero of one of the early sagas. The Havelocks were of good standing in the county of Durham and might have been better than comfortably off but for a certain taste for speculation, which had caused an earlier Havelock to lose his fortune in the South Sea Bubble. Henry's father was a prosperous shipbuilder with a yard in Sunderland and they lived at Ford Hall, Monk Wearmouth, where the boy was born on 5th April, 1795, five years after his elder brother, William. His mother was the daughter of a leading Newcastle solicitor and, though she died when Henry was only fourteen, hers was the dominating influence in his life. Little is known of Mr. Havelock except that he had some of the family taste for speculation and that he found difficulty in getting on with his second son. Mrs. Havelock was a woman of deep personal piety, a devout Evangelical churchwoman, and she inspired the boys with her belief from their earliest days. It was her custom to summon them regularly to her room for Bible reading and prayer and, when she died in 1809, she had already bequeathed to Henry her untroubled faith and a disposition towards austerity and self-discipline. He was only five when they left Durham and moved to Ingress Hall, near Dartford, in Kent. As far as their material fortunes went it was not a prudent move, for the income from the distant shipyard in Sunderland began to fall off and Mr. Havelock's attempts to recoup himself on the Stock Exchange were almost consistently unhappy.

William and Henry began their formal education at the Seminary of the Rev. Mr. Bradley at Dartford, first as day-boys and later as parlour boarders. The only account that remains of their early school-days comes from John Clark Marshman, Henry's brother-in-law and earliest biographer, who published a life of him in 1860, only three years after his death at Lucknow. Marshman was an earnest Baptist and a sincere admirer, with a tendency to see all motives and actions from a sectarian angle. He seems to have accepted the old-fashioned convention of biography, which demands signs of coming greatness to appear during school days, and there is something naïve in his efforts to find them in Henry's.

He solemnly relates an incident when the boy fell out of a tree and felt no fear because, he said, he was only thinking of the apple which he was trying to reach, and there are the usual tales of his taking a beating instead of his friend and standing up against a bully on behalf of a smaller boy.

In 1805, when he was ten, Henry went on to Charterhouse and the story of his life there is a little more detailed. Charterhouse was no worse, but certainly no better, than any other big school, at a time when the life of the average public-schoolboy was about as comfortable and civilised as that of a convict. Discipline was severe, fagging incessant and punishment ferocious, but Henry seemed to thrive on it, and, if Marshman may be believed, he was one of the few boys of his time who looked back on their schooldays with real affection and gratitude. He said himself, in after life, that Charterhouse taught him the meaning of discipline. It seems probable that the rigours of life there were easily accepted by a temperament schooled by his mother's example and teaching to a Puritan belief in the beauty of austerity and the spiritual value of suffering. It is harder to believe Marshman's story that when Dr. Raine, the Headmaster, retired and was succeeded by Russell, a more enlightened and humane man, the consequent relaxing of some of the discipline was so unwelcome to Havelock that he persuaded his father to take him away.

One thing which Charterhouse gave to him, or at any rate fostered, was a taste for and a habit of reading. He became a competent, if not a profound classical scholar with a preference for Greek rather than Latin. He took with enthusiasm to Cæsar and Livy and especially to Thucydides. The story of a campaign always drew him, though he had as yet no idea of a soldier's career. His mother, whose wish was paramount with him, had early destined him for the Law, the profession of her own family, and there is no reason to believe that, at this stage, he thought of any other future.

It is not surprising that he should have studied the stories of the great campaigns, for he grew up at a time when war was a commonplace of the daily news. He was in his first term at Charterhouse when Trafalgar was fought, and, when he left, Napoleon's Grande Armée were just starting on their retreat from Moscow. He had, too, a closer link with contemporary history in his brother William, who was serving with Craufurd's Light Division in the Peninsula. The effect of Henry's classical reading was evident as soon as he himself joined the army. Even as a junior subaltern in the 95th, he was a voracious reader of military history, and when he began to write the accounts of his own campaigns, his love for Latin was evident in the awful dignity of his polysyllabic style. The preface to his first published work, the narrative of the war in Burma, is a formidable piece of prose which contains many allusions to Latin historians and a generous excerpt from Thucydides, in the original Greek, with no translation. Havelock's own English style is, at times, almost a caricature of his masters'. Few other serving soldiers would think of describing the setting up of camp by an advance party as 'previous castramentation'.

Another habit, which must surely date from his days in the upper forms at Charterhouse, was the persistent one of making a formal address to his troops before action. It was the 'contio' of the Roman generals, and he adopted it as soon as he got the chance, though he was never very successful as a speaker and it is on record that the Highland regiments under his command could never be induced to join in the cheers which his perorations invited.

Havelock maintained throughout his life at Charterhouse the habit of prayer and Bible-reading, which he had learned from his mother. The habit went with him into the Army, where it developed into a taste for preaching. Charterhouse was responsible for the name, 'Havelock's Saints', which was later to become familiar to the Army in India—first in scorn but, later, in tones of unwilling admiration. The prayer-meetings among the 13th Foot had their origin in a Charterhouse dormitory, where a band of boys under his leadership used to meet for prayer and for exposition of the Scriptures, the exposition being Havelock's self-imposed duty.

By the time that he was fourteen, and in his fifth year at Charterhouse, he had won a measure of respect from his fellows and the half-admiring nickname of 'The Philosopher' (or 'Phlos' for short).

In the same year the first deep grief of his life came to him, when his mother died suddenly of apoplexy. There were two younger sons now, but Henry was always the closest in spirit to his mother and the loss cast a gloom over what was left of his time at school. Her wishes were more than ever sacred to him now and she had always intended him for the Law, though he does not seem to have had any strong personal feeling either for or against it. He stayed two more years at Charterhouse and it was intended that he should go on from there to Oxford.

There seems always to have been a lack of sympathy between Henry and his father, and after Mrs. Havelock's death it increased. There was not enough money for Oxford, so Henry was entered at the Middle Temple in 1813, as a pupil of Chitty, the most famous 'special pleader' of the day. He was withdrawn after a year and the only explanation offered by Marshman is a 'disagreement' with his father.

There followed two miserable years of boredom at home, while he was trying to decide on a career, and it was now that his mind began to turn towards the Army. They were the years 1813 and 1814. In Spain, Wellington was fighting his way northwards and battering at the door of the Pyrenees. William Havelock rode with that army as a staff-officer in General van Alten's division and, later, was slightly wounded at Waterloo.

William came home on sick-leave and Henry, whose mind was now made up, begged him to help him to get a commission in a good regiment. There could be no question of purchase, but William had favourably impressed van Alten and willingly used such influence as he had with him. Van Alten exerted himself and in the autumn of 1815, Henry was gazetted as an ensign in the 95th Foot (now the Rifle Brigade). At the beginning of the following year, he reported for duty at their depot at Shorncliffe.

The non-purchase officer had to tread a long, hard road in the army of those days, especially when it was being reduced to a peace-time establishment. In war-time he could succeed to an officer killed in action, but in peace-time his only hope of escaping an interminable wait for a vacancy was to exchange into a regiment which was bringing up its strength before going overseas or when serving abroad. There were always a few purchase-officers who were not willing to serve overseas but who could not get a fair price for their commissions when they tried to dispose of them rather than go abroad. In such cases the regiments were made up to strength by the process called 'augmentation' and there were plenty of non-purchase officers ready to grasp the chance of promotion on transfer from their own regiments.

The iniquitous system of purchase was not finally abolished until the year 1867. Havelock suffered under it during almost the whole of his service and it is not surprising that he railed against it often and fiercely. Once, in a fit of anger, he swore that he had been 'purchased over by two fools and three sots'. He called himself bitterly, 'The neglected Lieutenant' and, in 1835, still a subaltern after twenty years' service, spoke of himself as 'a lieutenant of foot, without even command of a company and not a rupee in the world beside my pay and allowances'. It was to take him twenty-three years to become a captain and nearly thirty to become a lieutenant-colonel. He never commanded a battalion and, when at last he was gazetted as Major-General, he was sixty-two and had had forty-two years' service, thirty-four of which he had spent abroad.

The 95th Foot were a distinguished regiment and there were always plenty of applications for commissions and promotions from officers who could afford to pay the standard price or even more. Havelock saw at once that he could never hope to climb up more than a step or two on that particular ladder, but he had to stay with them at Shorncliffe for eight years before he found a chance of exchanging into another regiment with a gain in seniority. In 1823 the 13th Foot (later the Somersetshire Light Infantry) were 'augmenting' before leaving for India and Havelock exchanged into the regiment with which he was to spend most of the rest of his service.

His time at Shorncliffe was not wasted and he always looked back with gratitude on those years when, as he said, he 'now acquired some knowledge of his profession which was useful to him in after years'. (He had already fallen into the habit of keeping a diary in which he always referred to himself as 'he', disdaining the first person.) The habit of hard and steady reading which he had formed at Charterhouse was of great value to him now and he set himself to master all that he could of the theory of tactics and the history of his profession. He re-read the campaigns of Cæsar and Hannibal and added to them those of the great masters of European strategy, especially of the Emperor Napoleon and Frederick the Great. He studied the classics of war in Vauban, Lloyd, Templehoff and Jomini, and once at least managed to find the time and money to visit the continent and to make the tour of some of the famous battle-fields. When, in 1823, he sailed for India to join the 13th, he must surely have been one of the best-read and most knowledgeable subalterns in the Army.

CHAPTER

II

THE 13TH FOOT (1823)

TWO OF Havelock's brothers were already in the Army in India, William, the eldest, with the 4th Dragoons in Bombay, and Charles, the younger, with the 16th Lancers in Bengal. Henry sailed in the *General Kyd*, which also carried Major Robert Sale, who was on his way out to take command of the 13th, and who was to be the companion of many of his years of soldiering, and another officer of the regiment, Lieutenant James Gardner, with whom Havelock soon became friendly. Gardner was a man of great piety and, during the long and tedious voyage, the two subalterns discussed the mysteries of their faith and shared in prayer and Bible-reading. Havelock underwent on the voyage the experience which is commonly known to Evangelicals as 'conversion' and wrote of himself:

> 'It was while the writer was sailing across the wide Atlantic towards Bengal, that the Spirit of God came to him with its offer of peace and mandate of love, which, though for some time resisted, at length prevailed. Then was wrought that great change in his soul which has been productive of unspeakable advantage to him in time: and, he trusts, has secured him happiness in Eternity. . . .'

Of Gardner he writes:

> 'The *General Kyd* also carried out a humble unpretending man, James Gardner, then a lieutenant in the 13th Foot, now a retired captain, engaged in home missionary work, and other objects of Christian benevolence, at Bath. This excellent person was most influential in leading Havelock to make public avowal by his works of Christianity in earnest.'

Gardner was able to expound to him much which he had found puzzling in his faith and, in return, he instructed Gardner and some of the other young officers in Hindustani, since he had included Eastern languages among his military studies at Shorncliffe.

They landed at Calcutta in May 1823 and found the 13th in barracks at Fort William, where Havelock shared his quarters with Gardner. It was now time for him to make the public avowal of which he had spoken and it must be admitted that at first his methods astonished and disgusted the 13th. He had not been with them for many weeks when he began to form one of the leagues of prayer with which he had startled Charterhouse. He sought out the religiously minded men in the ranks of the regiment and gathered them together at regular times for prayer-meetings, at which he expounded the scriptures. Not unnaturally his fellow-subalterns resented this activity by a newly joined officer and reacted to it in much the same way as had his contemporaries at school. The derisive name of 'Havelock's Saints' was heard again and he had to endure not a little ridicule and unpopularity. Neither was a new experience for him and he went on his way, ignoring the gibes, satisfied if he could help and win the souls of the men in the ranks. The senior officers, men of experience and thought, watched him with the men at work and at ease, and soon began to realise that his odd methods had much to recommend them even from a military point of view.

Once when the 13th were in camp for the night there was an alarm and the bugles sounded to rouse the men, but, as was their custom whenever possible, most of them were too drunk to answer the call, and Sale rode on to the parade-ground to find that more than half of the battalion were absent and that most of those present were barely able to stand up. It was not a sight to please any commanding officer, though in those evil days it was not uncommon, and Sale shouted lustily for the few men on whom he knew that he could rely to be sober and awake. 'Send for Havelock's Saints!' he bellowed across the parade-ground. 'For God's sake, send for Havelock's Saints. You never see a Saint drunk when he ought to be on duty.'

The beginning of Havelock's ministrations in the 13th was also the beginning of his unceasing crusade for temperance in the Army. Drink was the curse of the British Army at that time and especially of the regiments on foreign service. It is difficult for those who only know the sober Army of today to realise the extent to which the Army of a hundred years ago was rotten with drunkenness. It was the cause of nearly all military crime and of those excesses which too often disgraced the army's capture of a town or a fortress. Over and over again, after an assault, the men rifled the cellars and spirit stores and drank themselves helpless or into a frenzy in which they raged through the streets, killing, raping, looting. Savage punishment was no deterrent. Neither the lash nor even the rope could keep the soldier away from his liquor. The Army was even so callous that in foreign towns it allowed the Commissariat to buy on contract the cheapest possible variety of locally brewed spirit—vile concoctions like arrack, which drove men half-mad and rotted their intestines, firewater made from rice or potatoes, which destroyed the younger soldiers used, up to a few weeks before, to nothing more deadly than English ale.

Henry Havelock had not only studied campaigns and the theory of war during those years in Shorncliffe. He had watched the private soldier and the N.C.O. and pondered their problems in the light of his own upright mind and Christian heart. He was a believer in discipline, as he had been at Charterhouse, but still more in self-discipline and he was too much of a realist to expect self-discipline from men who were treated, housed and fed like beasts. From the moment when he joined the 13th, he set himself to improve the lives of any men in the regiment with whom he could get into personal touch. As a Christian, his first approach was through his religion, but he was never the sort of Christian to overlook the needs of the body or the extent to which the spirit could be harmed by boredom, neglect and ill-treatment. His prayer-meetings appealed to the spirit and their aim was so to strengthen it as to enable the men to resist temptations. But he knew that the spirit of man is so weak that it needs every possible help in its battle with the Devil and that any honest effort to remove the temptation is of value, since in the greatest of all prayers, the Christian's entreaty is 'Lead us not into temptation'.

When, later, he became adjutant of the regiment he took practical steps to provide some attraction to lead men away from the taverns. It involved him in rather more ridicule than had his prayer-groups and for a while his startling innovation of the regimental coffee-house was the talk and the derision of India. He started modestly enough with a small building in the barracks of the 13th Foot, a place which was to be quiet and orderly and cleanly, where men could be served with mugs of coffee at a small cost, and where, he hoped, they would be able to get a little peace and privacy. It was the tiny seed from which was to grow so tremendous a crop of good for the private soldier—the Dry Canteen, the N.A.A.F.I., the army services of the Y.M.C.A. and Talbot House all owe something of their existence to the little building in the barracks at Kurnaul and to the subaltern from whose brain the idea sprang.

CHAPTER
III
THE BURMESE WAR (1824–1826)

WHEN Lord Amherst took over the Governor-Generalship of India from Lord Moira in August 1823, he inherited a credit balance in the accounts, which was a novelty, and an awkward situation in Burma, which was not. The difficulty with the King of Ava, the paramount power there, had been an intermittent irritation ever since the end of the previous century. The Kings of Ava had established an ascendancy over the other petty chieftains of the country and held Assam, Cachar and Arakan. Lately they had begun to cast covetous eyes on several islands off the Burmese coast, especially Shahpuri, a British possession near to the mouth of the river Naaf.

In January 1824 two Burmese columns invaded Assam and Manipur and beat off a small British force who were sent to turn them out. A few weeks later they went further and seized the island of Shahpuri. This was more than the British could stand and, in February, Amherst declared war and ordered Sir Edward Paget, the Commander-in-Chief, to prepare a force to chastise the Burmese for their impudence. It was to consist of two divisions, with attached troops, and the Presidencies of Bengal and Madras were each to provide one division. Sir Willoughby Cotton commanded the Bengal division, which included the 13th and 38th Regiments of Foot, the Buffs and seven battalions of native infantry. It was supported by two troops of British horse artillery and a light battery of camel guns.

Sir Edward's plan was for a water-borne expedition, which was first to take Rangoon and then to advance up the Irawaddy river, using a small flotilla as its base and line of supply. This was made easier because he had decided that it was unnecessary to carry any other supplies than ammunition, intending otherwise to live off the country. It was an economical arrangement which ignored the fact that they were to start at the beginning of the rainy season and that most of the countryside would soon be an impassable swamp. Medical stores were also overlooked, though the country was notorious for malaria and every sort of fever.

The army of Burma was under the command of Sir Archibald Campbell. Havelock was attached to his staff, but the ship in which he sailed was at least a week late and he did not join the Army until after the first troops had landed at Rangoon.

The British had been deluded into the belief that the Burmese hated the King of Ava and would rise in mass to support a liberating army. But the King of Ava was a thorough and experienced tyrant and had made provision against any such emergency. He drove away the inhabitants of any district which the British were likely to enter, after having first made them destroy their houses and crops and carry off all their movable property. The men were compelled to join the defending force and their wives and children were held as hostages for their good behaviour in the field.

The first troops to arrive in Rangoon were greeted by a few perfunctory shots from some antiquated fortress guns, mounted on the walls, which were soon silenced by the flotilla's guns. They landed without any more opposition. The men had been excited by stories of the fabulous wealth and magnificent buildings of the city, but they stumbled ashore to find, 'a vast assemblage of wooden huts, surrounded by a wooden stockade sixteen to eighteen feet in height.' A giant pagoda towered above a completely deserted city. The inhabitants had disappeared into the jungle, taking with them all the cattle and fowls and everything eatable that had been in the city. It was a discouraging reception for an army which expected to live off the country and had been looking forward to a rapturous welcome from its people. But, if all the food had vanished, there was plenty of drink to be had for the taking. The liquor stores were full and unconcealed and the army fell on them with delight. It seems probable that the stores had been deliberately left open and well-stocked, for the British soldier's addiction to drink was notorious and there was no surer way in which to undermine his discipline.

That first night in the city was a proof of Havelock's faith in abstinence for men on active service, though he arrived too late to see it. The men looked out over the desolate streets and beyond them to the swamps and the sodden jungle and the loneliness and strangeness of it all struck deep into sinking hearts and empty bellies. They forgot all discipline and broke their ranks to look for food and plunder. A day and night of drunken orgy passed, while the officers looked on helplessly. Before nightfall, most of the men were fighting drunk on the vile spirits which they had looted. It is to Campbell's credit that, by the time that Havelock's ship arrived a few days later, he had restored discipline and set the men to work. His first task was to put Rangoon into a state of defence and to find some supplies for his men. Since there were as yet no crowds to welcome their liberators with gifts of food, he ordered the troops to forage for themselves and sent strong parties out of the city to search the surrounding country.

Too many of them returned empty-handed. The Burmese in their retreat had swept the country clear of every form of food which could be moved or destroyed. The 'scorched earth' policy had been carried out with such remorseless thoroughness that Havelock and officers like Major Snodgrass, who knew their campaigns, compared it to the devastation of Russia in 1812 in front of the invading French. One enterprising battalion collected nearly 4,000 bullocks and were deeply incensed at being made to restore them to their owners. But the theory was that the British were not looters and that they had come to liberate the unhappy Burmese not to rob them.

Campbell of course reported the miserable position of affairs to the C.-in-C. India, but communications were slow overland, where they were beyond reach of the primitive telegraph, and by sea they were at the mercy of wind and wave. Some supplies began to arrive in a few weeks and with the first of them came the leaders of that flight of thieving civilian contractors, who battened on the distress of the soldiers and made a shameful profit out of the fighting man's misery. They had been in evidence in the Peninsula, where Wellington had spoken strongly in favour of hanging a few of them. They came now to Rangoon, offering eggs at five shillings each, beer at five pounds a case, stinking meat and rotten fish at famine prices. They knew that the army must pay their prices or starve. The officers, who had money, cursed them but they paid. The men, who had no money, starved. Rangoon had been occupied on the 11th of May, and it was well that Campbell had seen to his defences for a series of harassing attacks began almost at once from the dense jungle which came nearly up to the outer wall of the city and provided good cover for the Burmese. There was no attempt at an assault in force but the constant pinpricks preyed on the men's nerves and inflicted a few casualties. The Burmese were ill-equipped with fire-arms but they were expert shots with the bow, and more than one careless sentry fell with an arrow in his body. Anything on a bigger scale was unlikely, unless the enemy could bring up guns of a calibre heavy enough to breach the walls, and what few of these they possessed were in position for the defence of Ava. So for a short time the garrison stood on the defensive behind their walls, repelling the attacks without difficulty, but perpetually on the alert and growing hungrier all the time. Havelock had taken up his staff duties by this time and, after his fashion, began at once to see what he could do to help and comfort the men. It was not long before he seized on the Great Pagoda as ideal for his purpose. An officer who served in the expedition has told the story of how, one evening, he passed the Pagoda and heard coming from it the unmistakable sound of a Christian hymn. Curiosity moved him to look inside and, after threading his way through a labyrinth of passages, he came to what he described as 'a sort of side chapel, with images of Buddha in the usual sitting posture arranged round the room'. There was a tiny oil-lamp on the lap of each figure and, by their dim light he could see the scarlet coats and yellow facings of the men of the 13th, with Havelock in the middle of them.

He could pray with the 13th but he was not allowed to fight with them, when, a week after the invasion, the first sorties went out to probe the jungle for their enemies. Campbell had ordered a series of these attacks to test the enemy's strength and to deny to them any feeling that all the offensive spirit was on their side, and because he knew that his men would be in better heart if they could go out and attack the enemy. A party of the 13th was detailed for the first sortie on 19th May, and Havelock, who had not yet been in action, was determined to go with the men of his own regiment. Unfortunately, he was seen by a senior officer as he made his way as unobtrusively as possible towards the 13th's forming-up line and curtly told to get back to his office duties at Headquarters. It was a great disappointment to him, but he was a man of persistence and before the end of June he succeeded in accompanying the 13th on another sortie.

The first few attacks achieved little and caused some loss to the British, though the feeling of being on the move and attacking did much to restore morale. Most of the casualties at that time must be attributed to the careless methods of reconnaissance which were common throughout the whole British Army. In this campaign they were more careless than usual, because they made the fatal but not uncommon mistake of underrating their enemy. The Burmese were far from formidable in the open, but behind their peculiar type of fortification they fought bravely and skilfully. Their muskets were primitive and scarce, and most of their forces were divided into equal bodies of bowmen and spearmen, rather after the manner of the mixed units of musketeers and pikemen of the Thirty Years War. Above all they were proficient in the art of concealment and in digging themselves in, a task which the British soldier has always regarded as a fatigue to be avoided at all costs. The Burmese used the type of trench which is known nowadays as a 'fox-hole' and their skill and speed in making them were astonishing. Moreover, they knew the country and most of them were half clad or nearly naked, so that they moved twice as fast and a hundred times as quietly as the heavily clad infantryman, under his load of ammunition and his haversack, wearing his woollen uniform and heavy boots.

The most formidable defence of the Burmese was the stockade, which might be anything from a small outpost to a forest fortress, capable of holding several thousand men. They were always well hidden in the jungle and were works of great strength, in a country where heavy guns could rarely be dragged near enough to destroy them. The stockades were square or circular erections, made from tree-trunks lashed together with creepers and filled in with thorn bushes and brushwood, with the added protection of ditches and pointed stakes. As they were always well sited and hidden, the army usually discovered them by blundering straight into them and their first warning was a flight of arrows or a volley of musket shots. Behind these defences the Burmese fought tenaciously, the more so for the knowledge that any failure on their part would be expiated by their womenfolk in unspeakable tortures.

The most formidable of these stockades was the gigantic one at Kemmendine, some miles upstream from Rangoon, and on 1st June Campbell moved out in force to attack it by land and water. The result was a complete failure and cost the attackers 120 men killed and many more wounded. The attack was, as usual, delivered with hardly any previous reconnaissance and the troops, who should have encircled the objective, lost their way in the dense jungle and fired into each other. But they were learning their lesson and less than a week later another attack was mounted with much more care and with the result that the 13th and two Native regiments carried the position.

Havelock was present at both of these attacks and in July found himself in the unexpected position of commanding one. It was his first experience of commanding troops in the field and not a happy one. He was attached to a party which had been sent out to assault one of the smaller stockades. He wrote a vivid account of the experience to his friend Gardner, who had been left behind at the depot in India:

'The senior officer, who had just risen from a sickbed, was exhausted by fatigue, and unable to act, and I, as the only staff officer present, seized the reins at rather a critical moment. The troops did not support me, as older soldiers would have done: not that they evinced any desire to go about, but they stood about, wasting ammunition in an exposed position, when they should have pushed en avant and used their bayonets, as I bid them do. I had sixteen of my friends of the 13th killed and wounded, and poor Barrett's right arm shot off. After this, my pioneers (Madrassees) fairly flung down the ladders and would not budge, though I coaxed, harangued and thrashed them by turns.'

He was at it again three days later in what he calls 'a grand field-day of stockades, the best which the force has made'.

That was to be Henry Havelock's last day of fighting for some time, for in July he fell a victim to the great wave of sickness which swept through the troops at Rangoon, till nearly half of them were either dead or in hospital by the end of the month. The rainy season was at its height and dysentery and fever raged among the ill-fed men in that insanitary city. There was an outbreak of cholera and for a while it was all that the exhausted army could do to maintain its grip on the small stretch of country which it controlled, against the incessant counter-attacks of the Burmese. Havelock escaped the diseases which destroyed his comrades but he suffered from so severe an attack of some rare liver trouble that the doctors were mystified and could do nothing but ship him off to Calcutta. The doctors there were of as little use and tried to persuade him to apply for a year's sick leave and return to England. He refused, since it would mean, in his opinion, that he would be able to take no further part in the campaign and lose the chance of a step in rank by brevet or permanently, to replace an officer killed in action. He was desperately keen to get on in his profession and, as a non-purchase officer, he could not afford to neglect any chance of active service. He pleaded to be allowed to substitute a short journey by sea to Bombay, though, at the rate at which the campaign was proceeding, he might have taken his full year and still been in time for the end of it.

As a matter of fact it was nearly a year before he rejoined the army. He was not well enough to leave Calcutta till January 1825, when he embarked for Bombay. The voyage, good feeding and relief from strain did him good and he was able to enjoy his time at Bombay where he was most hospitably received by the Governor, Elphinstone, and the Commander-in-Chief, Colville. His brother was then at Poona with the 4th Dragoons and Henry spent several weeks with him before returning to Bombay, from whence, by way of Madras, where he spent a fortnight, he made his way back to Burma. He landed there in June and set out to rejoin the army at Prome, to which they had by now advanced in their thrust towards the capital, Ava. He found them in better heart and health, reinforced and receiving regular, though not generous, supplies from the Commissariat. At last some of the inhabitants had come to the conclusion that the British might turn out to be the winning side, and some of the welcome for which they had vainly looked the year before began to greet them as they moved up country. Presents of fruit and game from the natives were a welcome addition to the mess-tables, though, as Havelock characteristically remarked, 'this does nothing for the true object of an officer's care, the strength of the private soldier'. He took part in the closing battles of the campaign at Napadee and Patanago and in the last of all at the end of the year, when the last reserve of the Burmese, the 'Retrievers of the King's Glory', 18,000 strong, came out to defend the capital and went down before the concentrated fire of Campbell's artillery. The King of Ava, realising the futility of further resistance, sued for peace, the terms of which were agreed upon and signed at Yandaboo on 24th February, 1826. The King was forced to cede three provinces to the British together with an indemnity of a million pounds, and the treaty was to be solemnly ratified in his palace in Ava. Havelock was one of the officers appointed to represent Campbell at the ceremony at 'The Golden Foot', where he was annoyed to find that he had to remove his shoes before entering the royal throne-room. The proceedings were maintained at a uniformly high level of courtesy, as between two sovereign states, and each side loaded the other with handsome presents. The King was pleased to confer decorations on the officers who had attended and Havelock found himself entitled to wear a golden forehead fillet and to describe himself as a 'Valorous, Renowned Rajah'. He would, of course, have had to get the C.-in-C.'s permission to wear the decoration, but there is no record of his ever having applied for it, and, when the Army of Burma broke up to return to home stations, his appointment as D.A.A.Q.G. ceased to exist and the Valorous, Renowned Rajah returned to regimental duty as a subaltern in the 13th.

CHAPTER IV

HANNAH (1826–1838)

HE WAS thirty-one now, with eleven years of service and one campaign to his credit. Yet his chance of getting a captaincy seemed no nearer and he was beginning to feel anxious. He was as punctilious as ever about his regimental duties and his care for the men, but he had his own career to think about, and he needed money.

He needed it more than ever, because he had fallen in love with Hannah Shepherd Marshman, the daughter of a Baptist missionary at Serampore, sister of his future biographer. He had made her acquaintance in his first months in India, at Fort William, and he had kept up a correspondence with Miss Marshman's brother during the Burmese campaign. He could not hope to marry on a subaltern's pay and he saw bleak visions of the years rolling on while he still waited for his Company and his bride. Sir Willoughby Cotton, under whom he had served in Burma, had been impressed by the efficiency of this serious subaltern, who was a preaching fanatic and yet so stern a disciplinarian and so brave a fighter. Through Cotton's influence, he was able to get a temporary appointment as an interpreter, but the pay was small and there was no future in it. A few months later Cotton was appointed to command a brigade and Havelock went with him as interpreter, on a tour of duty which gave him his first sight of the town of Cawnpore.

By way of adding to his income—and also of expressing some of the views which he held very strongly about tactics—Havelock determined to write the history of the Burmese War and to get it published in India. He was shrewd enough to know that, unless it came out quickly, it would not survive the brief interest which the war had attracted and he wrote often and urgently to Marshman at Serampore for his help in getting the book through the press.

> 'It would not, I presume, occupy many weeks to get it through the press at Serampore. Public curiosity will not demand more than 300 copies. . . .

> Tell me what you think of the state of public opinion in India. Do the Indian community care one straw about the Burma war? Do they care enough to read 300 pages about it?'

He soon found out that they did not. Anyone who could read three, let alone 300, pages of his turgid prose would have to care very deeply indeed about his subject. Havelock was a gay and amusing correspondent when he was writing a letter to a friend but, when he embarked on a serious work, he seemed to be trying to copy his beloved Cæsar—even to the extent of referring to the enemy as 'The Barbarians'. His preface alone was enough to discourage the casual reader if only on account of the long extract from Thucydides. He was meticulous in his instructions for the form and arrangement of his work and sent an anxious request to Marshman to correct a quotation from the *Iliad*, as he had no copy of it by him and had quoted from memory. Marshman did what he could to help, but he was unhappy about the possible effect on Havelock's career of his extremely outspoken criticism of the conduct of the campaign. He suggested this to Havelock, who had already thought of it for himself.

> 'I am half afraid [he wrote] of the storm of hostility which the free discussion of recent events might bring on a subordinate officer. Men of years and rank are so unwilling ever to be proved in the wrong. And I cannot in common honesty attempt to show that in 1824, '25 and '26, they were always in the right.'

In a later letter he even goes so far as to admit that

> 'The Generals I have not treated quite so well. As regards them, I shall perhaps have to modify and soften down, before I can venture to print. . . . But, were the manuscript carried through in statu quo, it is not impossible that I might find my name omitted in the Army List of some subsequent month for having presumed to think that a Brigadier-General can do wrong.'

He was beginning to know his seniors, though he was prepared to take a reasonable risk of annoying them and plainly he did not 'modify and soften' nearly enough. He had expected criticism but he was honestly surprised when, on publication of the history, he found himself to be about the most unpopular subaltern in India.

Echoes of the trouble even spread to distant England and penetrated into the War Office. His brother William, some time afterwards, while on a visit to England, called at the Horse Guards and was confronted with a copy of the book and a demand to know whether he had written it. On his denying authorship and mentioning his brother

Henry, he was rewarded with the chilling remark, 'Your brother, you say? Then I take it he is tired of his commission.'

Fortunately for Henry—or had he for once been tactful?—one officer who did not seemed to be disturbed by the book was Cotton. It was doubly fortunate because Cotton was one of those officers who are obviously marked out for greater things. Havelock soon had proof of his goodwill, when Cotton offered him the adjutancy of the newly formed depot for The King's Troops in India, at Chinsura. The troops which were sent out from England as replacements and reinforcements for the units already serving there had always presented a problem because there was till then no central depot to which they could report and where they could be assembled and given preliminary training, before being despatched to join their units. A draft for a battalion of foot might arrive at Calcutta, to find that their unit had been sent into the Punjab or on to the North-West Frontier and, since there was nowhere where they could be held, they had to be sent on at once. The depot at Chinsura was an excellent innovation but, like many of its sort, it failed to survive an economy drive on one of those too frequent occasions when a spendthrift government tries to repair its extravagance by starving the Army. At least it served to give Havelock temporary employment at a higher rate of pay, and it also made it possible for him to pay frequent visits to the Marshmans at Serampore. Both he and his Hannah were getting older, and they felt that they could not wait much longer for each other. Havelock had of course no inkling of the abrupt way in which the depot would be abolished and he could reasonably expect it to employ him until he should get his captaincy. So on 9th February, 1829, they were married at Serampore.

It was characteristic of him that even on his wedding day, his military duties took precedence. He was due to sit on a court-martial that day in Calcutta and, though any fellow-subaltern would gladly have stood in for him, he felt obliged to attend the court. He left immediately after the ceremony, drove hurriedly to Calcutta, performed his duty, and drove back again to reach Serampore in time for dinner. His brother-in-law thought it admirable. What his bride thought remains her secret.

Hannah Havelock was a missionary and a member of a family of missionaries and she understood duty and sacrifice. But she was also a gay, loving woman and to her was revealed the inner Henry Havelock who was so different from the stiff, preaching martinet whom the army knew. His letters to her were and always remained as tender and amusing as his historian's style was pompous and turgid. He had not made many friends so far in his career, because he was necessarily, as well as by temperament, absorbed by the effort to get on in his profession, and he had never been able to afford to join in the shooting parties, the race-going or the balls with which the other subalterns beguiled their time off duty. He was not, at this time, a total abstainer by conviction but even an occasional glass of wine in the Mess was a strain on his finances. His contemporaries thought him a crank, or at best a dull dog, and excluded him more and more from any but formal contacts and from the lighter side of their life, so that he had often been very lonely.

He had a great capacity for love and Hannah released it. He was at his ease with her, he could relax and know the infinite relief of a man who all his life has to be on his best behaviour because he feels that he is always on his trial. No one who reads the letters which passed between husband and wife during his many enforced absences can doubt that theirs was a loving and happy married life. Like so many apparently lonely and shy men, Havelock was devoted to children and his own were a great happiness to him. Their first, a girl, was born in 1830, but only lived for six years. In 1836, when the regiment was at Kurnool, Mrs. Havelock had gone with the girl and her younger brother, then aged five, to the hill-station of Landour, where they had a bungalow. One night the native servants ran out of their quarters and gave the alarm, when they saw flames leaping from the roof and playing round the wooden walls. They got Hannah out, but the little girl was dead and for weeks Hannah's life was in danger. It was only two years since the third child, the boy Ettrick, had died in infancy, and the double tragedy, together with the injuries which she had received from falling timbers, nearly killed her. Only she knew how her husband's love and the tenderness of his nursing snatched her back to life. The second child, a son, had been born in 1831 and called Henry, and their pride and joy in him were intensified by the unhappiness in the loss of the others—and, as he grew up, for himself and his own personality and achievements. He grew to be just such a son as they would have had by choice—as brave a soldier and as true a Christian as his father but with a dash and gaiety which were all his own. Havelock's letters show what anxious thought he gave to the boy's bringing up and it was his great happiness to have him as his A.D.C. on his last campaign, as it was Hannah's only comfort to know that, when her husband died in Lucknow, the boy was with him to the last.

Soon after his marriage, and almost certainly as a result of it, Havelock was devoting his thoughts to the sect from which he had taken his wife and among which were so many of his friends. He had been brought up by his mother's influence as an Evangelical Churchman, but he was drawn to his wife's faith and seriously thought of adopting it, and, being Henry Havelock, he did so only after a prolonged and careful reconnaissance. He discussed it endlessly in those hot days at Serampore and in the wonderful star-lit Indian nights, with Hannah and with her family. Strangely enough, as it seemed to him, they were not disposed to help him. Marshman, who tells the story and who took part in the discussions, asserts that they did not feel it to be their duty to make converts among the European population because they had been sent out to convert the Indian natives. So Havelock made his own decision. He accepted the Baptist faith and was baptised by the Rev. Dr. Mack at Serampore in the year of his marriage.

Characteristically, now that he was officially a Baptist, his first action was to apply on behalf of all the nonconformist fraternity in the regiment for leave to absent themselves from the Church of England parades on Sundays and to attend their own places of worship. The application was forwarded through the usual channels and was finally granted in 1839, roughly ten years after its first submission.

In 1831 the depot at Chinsura was no longer in existence and the Havelocks moved about the country with their regiment like any other soldier's family. They were first at Agra, then at Kurnaul and Dinapore. For three years they lived the quiet, uneventful army life, finding that it was just and only just possible to bring up a growing family on a subaltern's pay and allowances, but that it left no margin for anything else. Henry had been steadily working at his Eastern languages and was now qualified as a first-class interpreter in Hindustani and Persian, and a temporary attachment in that employment to the 16th Foot at Cawnpore brought them in a little extra money, but they were always hard up and sometimes near to poverty. Promotion still delayed and once, in despair, Havelock broke out with the bitter complaint, 'If something is not done soon, I must really live and die a lieutenant.' His need was so pressing and his feeling so strong that he made efforts to arrange for the purchase of his captaincy by negotiating for a loan with the Calcutta banking house of Alexander and Co. They were willing to help him and his spirits rose, only to be damped by Alexander and Co.'s sudden failure. After that he tried two other houses in Calcutta, but he must have been badly advised, for both the firms with whom he negotiated, Mackintosh and Co. and Fergussons, went bankrupt within a few weeks of each other. He was left contemplating a future which seemed bleak, but his bad luck could not hold for ever and in 1835 the adjutancy of the 13th fell vacant and at once he applied for it.

His old friend Robert Sale, who commanded the regiment, was glad to recommend him to the Governor-General whose approval had to be obtained for all such appointments. Lord Henry Bentinck was instantly besieged by a spate of letters from officers who had taken offence at Havelock and his religious practices. There were some of an astonishing venom and bitterness, but fortunately Bentinck had a mind of his own and knew both Havelock and his wife whom he had met while on a visit to Serampore. Hannah had been able to be of use to Lady Bentinck as an interpreter during the visit and now she plucked up courage to write to her in support of her husband's request. Lady Bentinck invited her to visit them and received her most kindly at Barrackpore Park. While they sat and talked, Bentinck came into the room holding a sheaf of papers which he showed to her. They were a selection from the letters from Henry's enemies, and he set her mind at rest at once by saying, 'Before I refer to this correspondence, I give you the assurance that I have bestowed the adjutancy of the 13th on your husband, because he is unquestionably the fittest man in the corps for it.' The letters were all pitched in the same key—Havelock was a fanatic: he lowered himself by consorting with the men on friendly terms: he would not show impartiality as adjutant if he were appointed: his conduct was not that of a gentleman—letters which reflected little credit on the writers, who were themselves officers and supposed to be gentlemen. But against them, on the credit side, were the records of his own men, as compared with the rest of the regiment, and the strong recommendation of Colonel Sale. Lord Henry Bentinck had no love for men who tried to blacken the character of a fellow-officer. His only comment on them was a gentle and half-smiling hint to Hannah, that, 'The Adjutant should not preach.'

No power on earth could keep Henry Havelock from his prayers and his preaching and now he had the chance of influencing not a half-company but a whole regiment and he grasped at it. The services went on, the coffee-houses were established at every cantonment and he formed a Temperance Society in the regiment, of which Colonel Sale became one of the first members. The next three and a half years, during which he held the adjutancy, were a busy time and Bentinck had no cause to regret his decision. Between them, Sale and Havelock brought the 13th up to a pitch where they were acknowledged to be the most efficient and least troublesome regiment in India. Havelock was a man who counted his blessings and was duly grateful for them.

He reckoned it not the least of them that he had failed to arrange a captaincy by purchase a few years before, since it came to him in the ordinary way of a vacancy in 1838. He was grateful but could not help a feeling of regret for having to give up the adjutancy in order to take a company. It was only natural that he should feel it, but, being what he was, he took himself to task for what he thought of as ingratitude. He wrote to Marshman:

> 'But how soon do the germs of discontent spring up in the corrupt human heart. I am ready to repine, did not faith forbid. 1st. Because I have only got advancement at last by the death of a dear friend: 2ndly, Impatience suggests that, as things stand, it would have been better that I should not have been promoted till this war were over. [It was the year 1838 and war in Afghanistan was almost certain.] As Adjutant I should have taken a great interest in the discipline and conduct of my corps. I hope I may not take less as a captain: but as regards the field of exertion, a captain is nearly as absolute a cypher as a lance-corporal: not so an adjutant.'

The rumours which were flying about barracks and Mess were true. England was blundering into war with Afghanistan and soon it was certain that the 13th were to go and that Sale was leaving the command of the regiment to take up a brigade. Sale's first wish was to have the adjutant, who had done so much for him, as his brigade-major and put in a strong request for him, but Sir Henry Fane, who had just succeeded to Combermere's command in chief, appointed another and very senior officer.

> 'Sir Henry Fane [Havelock wrote] has given the place to the claims of an older captain who had served in the Peninsular War. I have no right to repine at this, but cannot help seeing that the safest rule is to allow commanders to select those whom *they* esteem fittest for the work.'

He reconciled himself to making the campaign as a company commander, and his chief thought was for his wife and family. Henry, the eldest, was seven now and there was Joshua, the younger brother. It was time for education to begin, especially for Henry who was already destined for the Army. Havelock wrote:

> 'The nearest thing to my heart of all earthly things is the education of my boys. Mack is coming out. Will he, can he be persuaded to take Harry in hand, and fit him for the Military College? My views regarding the boy know no divarication. I have one object—that he should be taught Greek enough, in which I have already entered him, to read the New Testament in the original and be well crammed for Sandhurst.'

Mack, the missionary who had baptised Havelock, had been home on leave and reached India at the end of the year. He at once agreed to take the boys in hand and initiated a rigorous course of the classics with the addition of some mathematics.

Havelock had thus solved the most urgent of his personal problems and was able to give his mind to his preparations for the coming war. His main anxiety was the physical condition of his men for, in July and August, the regiment had suffered heavily from fever and cholera, so that they were under strength and there were too many unfit men in the ranks. No new drafts were on the way to join them, though, had there been any, they would have been of little use in warfare in a savage country against such an enemy as the Afghan.

Havelock was busy with clothing and equipment, with musket and bayonet drill, when he was summoned by an old acquaintance who had not forgotten him. Sir Willoughby Cotton, who had commanded the Madras troops in Burma, had seen in him a promising staff officer and now wrote to offer him an appointment as second Aide-de-camp in the division which he was to command, which was to consist of nine regiments. He would not need a second A.D.C. until the division reached the theatre of war and, for the time being, he proposed to employ Havelock as a temporary post-master. It was only a stop-gap and any purchase officer would have scorned it, but Havelock had his career and his living to make. He was too sensible to refuse any offer of employment which would lead to something better.

CHAPTER V

AFGHANISTAN (1838–1840)

IT WAS sheer ill-fortune that the Governor-General in 1839 should have been Lord Auckland, to whom the Russians were not only a threat but an obsession. He was the nephew of Lord Minto, lately a most successful Governor-General, with a particular fondness for the North-West provinces and a keen eye for Russian influence. Auckland was anxious to maintain the standard which his uncle had set during his term of office, but he lacked the gifts, the sure judgement of men and the large view of events, which had been Lord Minto's attributes. Russia preyed upon his mind and gave him no rest. So, when reports came of Russian attempts to win over Afghanistan and were followed by Persian troops marching on Herat, Auckland ran to meet trouble, not half-way but up to the frontier. Herat was an outlying possession of Afghanistan and was ruled by a brother of Dost Mohammed, the King of that country. The Persians had always coveted it and in 1838 they invaded the country and invested the city. It was not of great importance to anyone in India, or even of much interest to anyone except Auckland, always alert for the Russian threat. More serious was the news that Russia was making diplomatic approaches to Dost Mohammed in Kabul. Captain Burnes, one of the most famous travellers of his day, had been sent to Kabul as a special envoy. He, if anyone, might have been supposed to know how things stood there, and he was not alarmed. Dost Mohammed, he was convinced, wanted no dealings with Russia if only for the reason that he knew that the Russians were partly oriental like himself, and therefore unlikely to make such fair bargains or to keep them as faithfully as the English. In fact, though a Russian envoy had arrived in Kabul, Dost Mohammed was not interested enough in him to give him an audience. Count Vicovich was an unimpressive figure, an envoy from *opera buffa*, described as wearing long black kid gloves and carrying a French translation of Burnes's book of travels and 'a letter thickly powdered with gold-dust, written in Persian and purporting to come from the Court of Russia'. But Auckland took him more seriously and to some extent he was influenced by other officers of the political service who disliked and were jealous of Burnes. His pre-occupation with Russian spies led him to decide on an attempt to relieve Herat before the Persians could take it from Afghanistan and the Russians from Persia. He determined, too, that it would be in Britain's interest to have on the throne at Kabul another ruler who was less likely to favour Russia. His mind turned to a certain Shah Sujah, who had ruled there a few years ago until Dost Mohammed had turned him out.

Shah Sujah, after some vicissitudes, was now living as a pensioner of the British at Ludhiana, on an income of 4,000 rupees per month, which barely enabled him to keep his fourteen sons, nineteen daughters and all their mothers in reasonable comfort. If Auckland were to restore him to the throne, he was likely to show his gratitude by faithful attachment to the British and by turning a cold shoulder to Russia. The fact that he was incompetent and disagreeable could not be allowed to weigh the scales against him. At all costs, Britain must have a solid block of allies all the way between Bengal and the frontier.

The Ameers of Sind were unreliable and they would have to be dealt with later. Ranjit Singh was reliable as long as it paid him to be and not a day longer. Havelock, who met him once in the following year, described him as 'a one-eyed man in the last stages of decrepitude', but Havelock was perhaps prejudiced, for 'The Lion of the Punjab' was no friend to the cause of temperance. Indeed he drank 'a special concoction of his own', which, Havelock was sure, the most hardened toper in the British Army could not have survived for seven nights in succession. Ranjit Singh drank it all day and most of the night, only leaving off to indulge other personal tastes which Havelock found even more distressing. But he had not been called the Lion of the Punjab for nothing. One-eyed and decrepit he might be, but he was not yet too myopic to see his own advantage, nor too senile to take advantage of it. While kindly sheltering the exiled Shah Sujah, he had managed to possess himself of most of the royal jewels of Afghanistan, including the famous Koh-i-noor diamond. And later, while Dost Mohammed was settling down and getting his bearings, Ranjit Singh had almost unobtrusively relieved him of the provinces of Peshawar and Kashmir. For all his taste for liquor and dancing girls he was a power to be consulted and humoured, for, in his own country, he was a strong and vigorous ruler and the master of an army

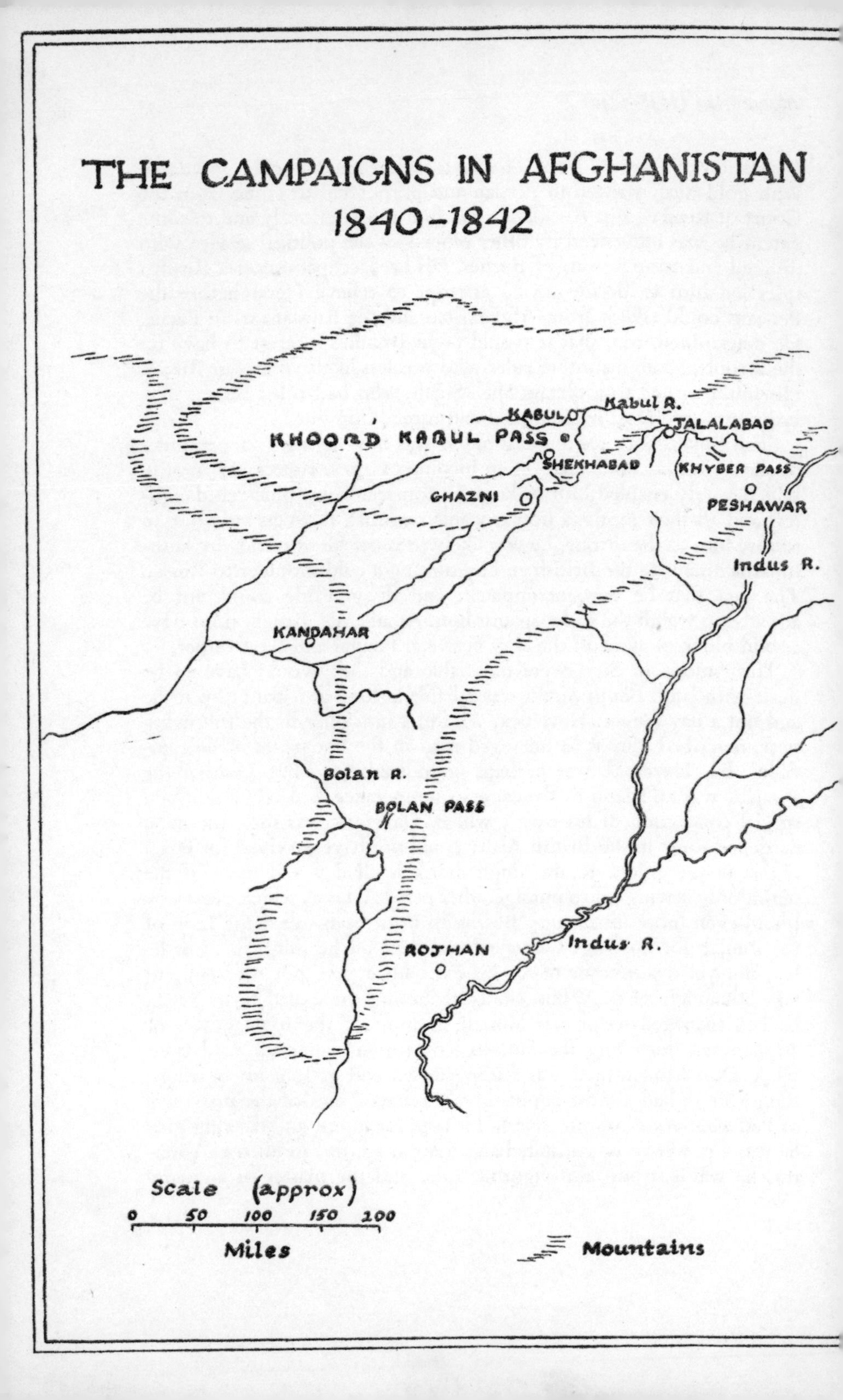

THE CAMPAIGNS IN AFGHANISTAN
1840-1842
KABUL
Kabul R.
JALALABAD
KHOORD KABUL PASS
SHEKHABAD
KHYBER PASS
GHAZNI
PESHAWAR
Indus R.
KANDAHAR
Bolan R.
BOLAN PASS
ROJHAN
Indus R.
Scale (approx)
0 50 100 150 200
Miles
Mountains

estimated at about 10,000 cavalry and 20,000 infantry, who had been trained by French officers, in addition to a horde of well-mounted and armed irregulars.

It was obvious to Auckland that Ranjit Singh must be, if not a party to a restoration in Afghanistan, at least favourable to it in theory. An invading army would have to cross the Punjab on its way to the North-West, and no army dare risk having an unfriendly force of that size across its line of communications. Fortunately Ranjit Singh was strongly in favour of the expedition, his long experience having taught him that when other men fought there were generally a few pieces of territory to be picked up by an astute and neutral onlooker, and that Britain wanted his help enough to make it worth his while.

So the original idea took shape in Auckland's mind and in discussion with the Council in Calcutta: and still more perhaps in informal talks with Macnaghten, one of the ablest and most ambitious of the political officers who were his advisers. Almost before they realised, the planners had committed themselves to an expedition on a full scale as for a war. Its task would be to relieve Herat, to replace Shah Sujah at Kabul on his throne, to overawe Sind and to strengthen the alliance with the Punjab.

It was an ambitious programme but no more ambitious than the military provisions for carrying it out. It involved the employment of two forces, one from Bengal and one from Bombay, with a rendezvous on the River Indus. To reach it, the Bengal force would have to march through 780 miles of rough country, most of which lay in the territory of what were at best rather doubtful allies. The Bombay force would come by sea to a point near the rendezvous and the combined forces would then face another march of 400 miles through hostile country to reach Kandahar, with a long distance yet to go to Kabul and Herat. Altogether it was a plan which obviously sprang from political rather than military thinking, but Sir Henry Fane, the C.-in-C. India, made no protest when he was asked to organise the expedition.

Fane was to command the army himself, with Cotton commanding the Bengal and Sir John Keane the Bombay contingents. Lord Auckland decided to accompany the C.-in-C. as far as the Punjab and there to meet and pay compliments to Ranjit Singh. Being an unmarried man, he took his two sisters and some of their friends with him.

Between them, Britain, Ranjit Singh and Shah Sujah arrived at a tripartite agreement, the terms of which were made public in Lord Auckland's manifesto of 1st October, in which, Sir Henry Durand says,

'The words "justice" and "necessity" were applied in a manner for which there is fortunately no precedent in the English language.' This is an historian's opinion, given after due reflection, but the reaction of fair-minded men at the time was no less unfavourable. Herbert Edwardes said that in the manifesto, 'The views and conduct of Dost Mohammed were misrepresented with a hardihood which a Russian statesman might have envied.'

The chief sufferers by it were the Ameers of Sind, who found themselves bound to pay tribute to Shah Sujah at the rate of 20,000 lakhs of rupees a year and the chief beneficiary was, it is hardly surprising to notice, the decrepit Ranjit Singh, to whom Sujah was bound to hand over 15,000 lakhs out of his twenty. It was to cost Auckland his reputation and Britain a crushing defeat.

Hardly had the manifesto been published than any necessity which might have been pleaded for the expedition ceased to exist, when, in November, the Persians raised the siege of Herat and withdrew from the country. Auckland might have saved the remnants of his honour by abandoning the scheme, but he was both weak and obstinate and Macnaghten and Burnes drove him on in their anxiety to bring off a spectacular diplomatic success. Macnaghten had just been appointed to the high-sounding position of 'Envoy and Minister on the part of the Government of India at the court of Shah Sujah-ul-Mulk'. Burnes had wanted it for himself, but he was junior to Macnaghten and had to content himself with the rank of Special Envoy. Auckland's idea was that Macnaghten should return to India as soon as Shah Sujah was safely on his throne, leaving Burnes to take over his position as British Minister at Kabul. As it turned out they both stayed there.

Auckland announced that the expedition would still go forward, 'with the view to the substitution of a friendly for a hostile power in the Eastern Province of Afghanistan, and to the establishment of a permanent barrier against schemes of aggression upon our North-West frontier'. He informed Sir Henry Fane, the C.-in-C., that in the circumstances a smaller force would be enough and that Shah Sujah's irregulars would lead the march, with the Bengal army following them. Such matters as the order of march are usually left to the commander to decide, and Auckland did not mend matters by adding, for Fane's information, some instructions about the part which Macnaghten proposed to play in the expedition. Fane was a soldier of long service and great distinction. He had commanded troops under Wellington and was not disposed to command a division under Macnaghten. He was a man who had no hesitation in speaking his mind about anything which affected the army, and he replied at once to the Governor-General:

> 'I do not think that for this my service is needed: and I consider Sir Willoughby Cotton quite competent to command. . . . I think, too, that your instructions to Sir William Macnaghten and to me are such as an officer of my rank could hardly submit to serve under.'

So Fane washed his hands of the whole proceeding, the more willingly that he was in very poor health and though he had only been out East for a short time was about to return to England and retirement. He decided to ride with them as far as the Indus, where he could take ship for Bombay and thence for England. He issued his orders for the transport and equipment of one of the maddest expeditions yet known in military history. Fortescue says of it that 'the experiment was as hazardous as that of displacing a Napoleon with intent to restore a Bourbon in France'.

Havelock, reading the orders and thinking as usual of his men, at once put his finger on the chief weakness, which he attributed, with some justice, to the fact that Fane had had no experience of war outside of Europe. The men had to march about twelve hundred miles, yet Fane's orders loaded them with equipment as though they were off for an afternoon's route march. It had always been the practice of the Army in India to have the men's personal kits carried behind the battalion on camels, which they hired at their own expense, or by native bearers, when camels were not available. Some of the expense was borne by battalion and regimental funds, but it was common for parties of men to club together and subscribe a part of their pay for the sake of greater ease and comfort. Fane was looking to the congestion which this practice would cause on the line of march, or else he did not realise how common was the practice.

> 'This rule was departed from [Havelock wrote] and the foot soldier directed to load himself instead of his camel, with his knapsack and a portion of his equipments, or necessaries as they are generally called. The European thus took the field carrying his firelock, ten pounds in weight, and his accoutrements with bayonet and sixty rounds of ammunition, thirteen pounds more. It was a question worthy of the fullest consideration whether it was advisable to load him with yet other thirteen pounds, in order to secure him the doubtful advantage of the constant possession about his person of his watch-coat, a pair of trousers, a shirt, a pair of boots and of socks, in fact a change of clothing, and his greatcoat, the latter being the only article with which he could not have dispensed.'

He adds that the native soldier was in a worse position as he was required to carry,

> 'an unga or undress tunic or short coat, a pair of trousers, a dhotee, or waist-cloth, a durree or small carpet, a tawa or iron utensil for cooking his uttah [flour] and a pair of shoes.'

Fane, in his orders, had specified a maximum of 14,000 camels. The Army took the road with between 29,000 and 30,000, nearly half of which carried the kits of officers and staff. Even the C.-in-C.'s staff, who should have set an example and seen to it that his orders were obeyed, clamoured for camels and yet more camels. Rumour in the Army said that Macnaghten alone needed sixty for his personal baggage. Fane, being new to Indian warfare, may not have known, but his staff should have warned him, that in the country ahead of them there was not one chance in a thousand of finding water to supply this multitude of animals as well as the horses of the cavalry and artillery. Major George Broadfoot, Havelock's greatest friend in the Army, wrote an account of the journey which he made a few weeks later, when he took a draft up after the main body. They started with 5,000 camels and lost 4,500 of them before they reached Kandahar, nearly all of them from death by thirst.

The first objective of the Army of Bengal was the River Gharra, on the border of the Punjab where they were to meet Ranjit Singh and hold a Durbar—a combination of compliment, conference and sheer revelry. Havelock, who was already thinking of writing a history of the campaign, took copious notes of all that happened on the march, and he was an indignant spectator of the arrival at their first camping-ground, west of Kurnaul. An advance party had gone forward to mark out the camping ground, so that each unit could march straight to its lines—the process which he used to call 'previous castramentation'. Unhappily these details were considered to be beneath the notice of the Europeans and left to the natives. 'Hindoostanee perversity', he remarks, 'had defeated all precautions. The camps were marked out, the lines for men and horses, baggage and stores distinguished by coloured flags,' but, 'the advance tents of the infantry had boldly steered for Liela Kheri, the first march of Brigadier Graham: the camels were found browsing and bewildered after their night's march, in the encampment of Sir Willoughby Cotton, and clamorous followers of the latter were shivering in the morning's cold, and lamenting their lost labour in the lines of General Duncan.' They had barely sorted themselves out by mid-day, losing half a day's rest, since they marched by night and slept in the heat of the day.

It was the inevitable confusion of an army gathered together from scattered units, lacking organisation into brigade or division and above all lacking a trained staff. It would improve as the march went on, but it was a disorganised force which straggled into the Grand Camp and saw Ranjit Singh's lines across the river. But at least they had arrived and were ready to enjoy his hospitality.

Ranjit Singh's hospitality was no light matter and it shocked Havelock to the depths of his Puritan soul. It began with the ceremonial meeting of the two chiefs of the armies and their staffs, all of whom were mounted on gorgeously decorated elephants. The elephants, starting from each side of an enormous parade ground, were urged on by the goads and shouts of their mahouts and met head-on in the middle of the ground. 'The shock of elephants at the moment of meeting', Havelock recorded, thanking God that he was not senior enough to be involved, 'is really terrific.' Fane must have been well coached in his duties, for as soon as the elephants met, he snatched Ranjit Singh out of his howdah and hauled him into his own. 'All this', Havelock explains, 'is managed amidst the roaring, trumpeting, pushing and crushing of impetuous and gigantic animals.' The officers and their mounts raced for the Durbar tent, which had been set up in the British lines and there dismounted at some danger to life and limb, not only from the feet of the elephants but from the muskets, with which the Sikhs were delivering an informal *feu de joie*. The Lion of the Punjab added a pleasing touch to the ceremony by falling over the trail of a howitzer outside the tent, to the obvious alarm of the Sikhs who thought that it was an ill omen, and to the disgust of Havelock, who thought that he was drunk.

On the following day Ranjit Singh gave an evening entertainment for his guests to which he was kind enough to invite the Governor-General's ladies and their friends, but, though he did his best to give them a good time, his idea of a cabaret show suitable for ladies did not commend itself to Havelock's more restrained taste.

> 'The time will [he wrote severely] it is to be hoped, come in India when national custom will be no longer pleaded as an excuse for the introduction, as on this occasion, of groups of choral and dancing prostitutes, for such these Kunchunees are known to be, into the presence of ladies of the family of a British Governor-General: or those of individuals of a nation professing to fence its morals with the securities of decorum. . . . It was the policy of the hour to humour and caress the old ruler of the Punjaub . . . but it was

> impossible not to feel that this complaisance was carried a little too far, when he was exhibited in the character of a Bacchus or Silenus, urging others to take part in his orgies, in the presence of English Gentlewomen.'

The Sikhs' display on the following day left Havelock with the reflection that 'on this, as well as on the opposite bank of the Gharra, there was not merely the infancy of military knowledge but its vigorous manhood'.

The ceremonies came to an end and the camps broke up. 'More serious avocations than fields', Havelock wrote, 'now demanded the exertions of the Army of the Indus.' Sir Henry Fane left for Bombay and home. The army went forward on the road which led to Kandahar and Kabul, and two years afterwards to the passes of the Khyber Hills.

CHAPTER VI

KABUL (1841)

IN MARCH 1840, when the reduced Army of the Indus moved forward, under the command of Sir John Keane, Havelock rode with it as second A.D.C. to Cotton, who was commanding the Bengal division. Havelock was in poor health at the time, being troubled with what he calls 'intermittent fever'. He attributed it to the fact that lately he had been drinking wine, after a long period of total abstinence. His friends had warned him that his habits were too austere for active service, but he decided that they were wrong. 'Water-drinking', he wrote, 'is the best regimen for a soldier. From that time the "Pure Element" became once more my only drink.'

It looked like becoming the only drink of the whole Army too, since the sad news had gone round the lines that Dost Mohammed had abolished drink in the whole of Afghanistan, in accordance with the rule of Islam. He had been a backslider in this respect earlier in his life, but was now a reformed character, and, like many such, inclined to be hard on former fellow-sinners. So the army moved forward with diminished enthusiasm, little guessing that in a few months they would be fighting each other at the wells and waterholes for a few sips of the 'pure element'.

There was little enthusiasm for the expedition throughout the army. The officers were disgusted with Auckland's manifesto and with the overbearing ways of the 'Politicals'. The people of the country through which they moved were sullen though not yet actively hostile, and the Ameers were openly dissatisfied with Shah Sujah. Havelock describes him as 'a stout, middle-aged man, with a beard dyed black' and says that his manners were cold and repulsive. The chieftains came into camp to make their obeisance to him as their future ruler, but his position had already gone to his head, and he treated them with unconcealed insolence. He felt himself to be a man of substance again, since the British had raised his allowance to 25,000 rupees per month, which was to be doubled as soon as he crossed the Indus. But the British were beginning to wonder whether his return would be as popular among his own people as the Politicals had led them to expect. They had several plain warnings as the army drew nearer to Kandahar. The Khan of Kalat said openly to them, after his audience, 'You English may keep him on his throne for a time, but as soon as you leave the country, Shah Sujah will be driven over the frontier.'

The army traversed vast tracks of sand and scrub where the water-holes were more than a day's march apart and there was no grazing for horse or camel. They were soaked by days of continuous rain, which chilled the men in their bivouacs and added to the weight of their load of equipment, and, now and again, they came across patches of lush vegetation which was too rich and green for the animals' empty bellies so that they suffered from colic. The cavalry horses especially began to lose condition, and the passing of the army was marked by the corpses of camels which had lain down exhausted and, being unable to rise, had been shot. There were violent storms of wind which enveloped the marching men and the camps in a whirlwind of sand, tore away guy-ropes and brought the heavy canvas down on top of sleeping men. Havelock, that seasoned campaigner, overcame the difficulty by appointing 'four of my largest and heaviest domestics' to hold down his tent, so that he slept peacefully 'till the cavalry trumpets sounded'. For a long time the Baluchis harassed them with sudden descents on the multitude of camp followers who always attended an army on the march in India. There would be a rush in the night, screaming in the unprotected suburb of the camp where the hangers-on slept, a slashing of long knives, and in the morning a huddle of dead men and a tale of camels stolen or hamstrung. There are more details of these troubles in the stories of other sharers in the march, officers such as Seaton and Broadfoot, than in Havelock's narrative, which confines itself to essential military movements, but once or twice he relaxes and gives a picture of the country and the men who crossed it, which is vivid for all its brevity.

'Headquarters moved on the 8th to Muhesir on the Bolon River. Never did the sun rise on a scene of more complete desolation than that which this part of Cutch Gundava presented to our view, when glimmering daylight first rendered the blaze of our torches no longer necessary. The tract between Rojhan and Burshoree was not more veritably desert. The cavalry and horse artillery had preceded us by a full hour: but we overtook in about that time their baggage and rear-guard, and a valuable escort of treasure confided to a detachment of them. There was something picturesque in the long strings of camels and the mixed and motley line of followers struggling along the sandy road over a brown and dusty plain on which nature seemed to have described the doom of perpetual solitude. . . . There were a few fields of green corn, in the immediate precincts of the place, a spectacle refreshing to the eye, wearied as it was with the gloomy sameness of the deserts which we had been traversing.'

A few days later, he records:

'When we were able to dispense with our torches, we found ourselves between two of the hills which we had observed to the northward the day before. They formed here a narrow pass, which was choked by a mass of led horses, camels, followers, carrying buenghees [baskets], doolies and palankeens, bullocks, mules and asses, troopers and suwars guarding portions of this train, the quadrupeds roaring, neighing, bellowing and braying and the bipeds growling, vociferating and abusing each other, and all struggling to get on.'

At last they came near to Kandahar—'non cauponantes bellum sed belligerentes' is his inevitable Latin tag—where they might have to fight, if Dost Mohammed should have given orders for it to be defended. The army had been on half rations for some time, the followers on less, and when they halted for the last time before reaching the town, they had only half-rations for two days left and the horses of the Bengal cavalry in particular had been so depleted that it looked as if the men would have to fight on foot. They had, Havelock calculated, marched 1,000 miles in 137 days. But, much to their relief, Kandahar was not held, though Dost Mohammed had ordered the garrison to resist. The British were very near with their guns and Dost Mohammed, terrible as he was, was far away in Kabul, and they had no stomach for a fight against heavy odds. They fled precipitately while the British were some way from the town, and took with them a long string of camels and baggage animals, loaded with the treasure which had lain there. The British attempted little or no pursuit, a fact which Havelock noted with disgust. True their horses were in poor condition, but it was an opportunity too good to neglect and he blamed Keane for his tardiness.

In Kandahar the troops were happy. It was like Paradise after the long and hungry marches. There was food in plenty, though they soon discovered that their worst fears were realised and that there was no liquor. The gardens were full of fruit and the market was there to supply their needs. Shah Sujah made a formal entry and there were the usual stately exhibitions of compliment and counter-compliment between him and the British, with much giving of presents. Shah Sujah, in a moment of expansion, admitted that he 'felt like a king at last'.

The officers found a trout-stream and went fishing while the men bathed and lounged and gorged themselves not altogether wisely on the abundant fruit. It was an idyllic interlude, but even in this Eden there was a serpent, as they found one night when two cavalry subalterns were brutally murdered. Lieutenants Inveraith and Willmer of the 16th Lancers had gone for a stroll outside the walls in the cool of the evening, when they were set upon by a gang of ruffians, slashed with the terrible Afghan knives and left to die on the path. Shah Sujah's 'Oh, gentlemen, you must be careful. This is not Hindustan' was cold comfort from one whose supposedly loyal subjects had done the murder.

The army dallied in Kandahar till 22nd July when Keane decided that it was time to take the next step towards Kabul. The fortress of Ghazni stood across their route and reports said that it was strongly held under the command of Mohammed Hyder Khan, one of Dost Mohammed's numerous sons and a fighter of some repute. Keane decided to send out a reconnaissance in force under the command of Sir Robert Sale. The main body followed on the next day and Keane took the much-criticised step of leaving his siege train behind in Kandahar. Apparently he did not set a high value on the strength of any Afghan fortification, but Havelock felt that he was taking an unnecessary and unjustified risk, since their little camel-guns and the 13-pounders of the Horse Artillery would be of no avail against troops who were strongly entrenched. Keane, remembering the difficulty of getting fodder and water for the animals on the march from the Indus, decided to take the risk, though, as Havelock thought, since they had dragged the guns for 1,000 miles, it was a pity to abandon them for the last eighty when there was a chance of their being of some use.

Sale's reconnaissance reported that Ghazni was very strongly held and that all the gates were bricked up so that no opportunity for a breach was presented, but Keane, reconnoitring himself with Havelock, discovered that the Kabul Gate in the north wall had been left unblocked, probably because the garrison expected reinforcement from that quarter. He determined to make his assault there. Since their light artillery would not be able to approach closely enough to have any real effect on the stout gate, the way to which was commanded by fire from the walls, he ordered a small party of Engineers to precede the assaulting force and to blow the gate in. It was a hazardous task for the party who would have to carry 900 pounds of powder, under fire, up to the gate, attach it and explode it with a fuse, but it succeeded. The assault was commanded by Sale and included the 13th Foot, whose colour was the first to be planted on the walls. After the first inrush of the assault, there seemed to be an undue delay, without any report being sent back, and Keane told Havelock to ride down to the gate and investigate. He was just in time to see Sale rolling on the ground, locked in combat with a huge Afghan and to hear him call out to another officer begging him to 'do him the favour of passing his sword through this infidel'.

The garrison defended bravely and the assault cost the British 17 in killed and 165 in wounded. The Afghans suffered far more heavily, losing 514 killed in battle and more than 1,600 prisoners, though Hyder Khan got away to fight again. Though the fortress had resisted and the rules of war still allowed its sacking by the capturers, the British behaved with notable restraint and clemency, which Havelock attributed solely to the absence of liquor in the town. 'Let me not', he wrote, in a mood of unusual diffidence, 'be accused of foisting in unfairly a favourite topic. But let it not henceforth be argued that distilled spirits are an indispensable part of the soldier's ration.' He adds, on the authority of the regimental surgeons, that the wounded recovered far more quickly for the fact that there had been no issue of a spirit ration for three weeks and that no drink was found in the town.

They rested for a week and then set out on the last stage of their journey expecting to meet really strong opposition before Kabul, but on 2nd August, when they were at Shekhabad, the welcome news came in that the army of Kabul had faded away and that Dost Mohammed was in flight. The Afghans had taken warning by Ghazni and, as was common in the country, treachery had been at work. No ruler of Afghanistan whose fortunes seemed to be on the wane could count for long on the support of his subjects, who always preferred unorganised banditry and raiding to pitched battles. So Dost Mohammed took horse and disappeared into the distant hills with a small party of his loyal friends. Keane sent a pursuit force of cavalry after him, under the command of Captain James Outram, but they soon lost touch in that wild, desolate hill-country, where their quarry knew every yard of the ground, and where every inhabitant, though he might not love the Dost, was an open enemy to the British.

Havelock witnessed the state entry of Shah Sujah-ul-Mulk into his capital on 7th August, accompanied by Burnes in 'a cocked hat fringed with ostrich feathers, blue frock coat with raised buttons, richly embroidered in collar and cuffs, epaulettes not yielding in splendour to those of a Field-Marshal, trowsers edged with broad gold lace'. All the officers were in full dress, the bands played, there was paying of compliments and giving of presents; and the Koh-i-noor gleamed in Shah Sujah's turban. (Ranjit Singh had died a few weeks before or it would surely never have returned to its former owner.) The King had come home to his own again and nothing was lacking but the plaudits of a welcoming people.

From them there was no response. They stood in the streets without a sound and with impassive faces watched him go by. There were not even any signs of hostility. They watched him as men watch an insect, something of no importance which is here this minute and will be gone the next. Havelock, watching them, came to the conclusion that 'the prevailing feeling was not one of much personal affection for Shah Sujah, who will probably, as a ruler, be less popular than the ex-Ameer.'

But in distant Calcutta and in more distant London the British triumph was unalloyed. Lord Auckland's statesmanship was acclaimed equally with the strategy of Sir John Keane, of whom Broadfoot had previously remarked that 'very few people knew him and those who did didn't like him'. Auckland became an earl, Keane a baron, Macnaghten a baronet. (He had been at Charterhouse with Havelock, but he was too important and too busy to notice a captain of foot.) Broadfoot was always apt to be critical of his superiors and an established reputation meant nothing to him. A short time later, weighing up the officers of the Army of the Indus, he reflected—after having dismissed everyone above the rank of colonel with contempt:

> 'We must come lower for good officers. First comes Captain Havelock of H.M.'s 13th Regiment. It is the fashion, especially in his own corps, to sneer at him: his manners are cold while his religious opinions (Baptist) seclude him from society. But the whole of them together would not compensate for his loss. Brave to admiration, admirably cool, looking on his profession as a science and, as far as I can see and judge, correct in his views.'

The march had been accomplished and they were there in triumph, but also in some bewilderment about the next move. Once the common urgency had ceased sectional interests began to intrude. The 'Politicals' were fully employed in trying to persuade the Afghans that they were glad to have Shah Sujah back again, and, as far as Macnaghten and Burnes—now Sir Alexander Burnes—were concerned, in trying to diminish each other's importance. The soldiers were busy with routine duties and, for a relaxation, with the unusually generous drink ration, and the senior officers were thinking of promotion.

Auckland had just announced, with considerable optimism, that, Shah Sujah being secured in power and the integrity of Afghanistan established, the British Army was now to be withdrawn. Sir Henry Fane, still nominally C.-in-C. India, was in Bombay and ready to leave for England, but no successor had yet been appointed and General Ramsay, the C.-in-C. Bengal, whose time had also expired, was anxious to be off. Cotton would then be the senior officer in Bengal and felt that he should be on his way back to Calcutta. In fact change was in the air and all the higher command felt that the sooner they were at or near the centre of army life and the source of promotion, the better for them. Definite orders arrived in November. The force at Kabul was to be reduced by the strength of a brigade, which was to return to Peshawar and have the duty of watching the passes through the hills. Sir Jasper Nicholls had arrived to take over the command at Calcutta, Cotton was to return to a divisional command in Bengal and Keane to leave Afghanistan and remain on the line of the River Sutlej. The court of Shah Sujah with the Headquarters of the Army of Afghanistan would withdraw to Jalalabad, which had generally been the Ameer's winter seat when Kabul became too cold for comfort. These orders were soon amended and Cotton was placed in command of all the forces in the district of Afghanistan, which included Kabul, Ghazni, Kandahar and Jalalabad, while Keane was to return to his command at Madras. The Court and Headquarters were to stay in Kabul. Havelock was naturally affected by the general feeling of unrest and had to consider his own position. Cotton was still willing to have him as A.D.C. with additional employment as an interpreter, but Havelock's old anxiety had returned when fighting ceased. He was only a captain, though he had hoped that, when honours were dropping like dew among his superiors, at least a majority might have descended on him. His boys' education had begun. Soon he would need more money for school bills, and he saw no prospect of getting it while he remained on Cotton's staff. His mind was once more running on authorship, in spite of the discouraging results of his last effort in that line after the campaign of Burma.

With that end in view, he had kept a detailed journal of the campaign, and Keane, to whom he had broached the idea, had encouraged him and had given him access to his own records. Havelock was convinced that, if the book were to do any good, it must be published at once, before the campaign had faded in memory, and that it must be published in England. He had been in correspondence about it with Marshman at Serampore, writing to him,

> 'I have once more commenced authorship and in a few weeks hope to have ready for the press "Personal Narrative of the Marches of the Bengal Troops of the Army of the Indus". I have determined to publish in London. Burnes, of whom I see much, and who is not going to publish himself, tells me that Murray would give a good price if the work were despatched speedily. The money is, of course, *now* the whole inducement. . . . An early sale is the thing to be desired, as *bare* lucre for my boys' education is the only object.'

Cotton alone was not in favour of the idea and was reluctant to release Havelock on leave for the winter and spring.

It was a difficult decision which Havelock had to make. On the one hand he had the opportunity of publishing his history and of making a little ready money—not a big sum, perhaps, but more than he could earn in many months' service. On the other, he would be cutting himself off from the army which was his life, so that he would be out of the way if promotion or employment should unexpectedly offer, and he might at any time incur the reproach of having left his duty for his own personal ends. He weighed all these things up and decided to take advantage of Keane's kindness. But he was never really happy about it either then or afterwards. When he arrived at Lahore on 30th December, he wrote to Marshman:

> 'I was long in doubt about it and at last decided wrong. From the moment when it was decided that Sir Willoughby should assume the command in Afghanistan, I ought to have made up my mind to remain there with him. Instead of this, swayed by the lesser motive of sending off my unfortunate publication to England, I have made a sad sacrifice of worldly advantage and military prospects: neither am I satisfied at all with the course I have taken as regards the claims of gratitude which Sir Willoughby had on me. . . . I have, by this step, lost my only military patron, my situation as Aide-de-Camp and a post as interpreter, which a day or two after was sanctioned by the Governor-General, a place made purposely for me. . . . I have never been fond of money, but my children need it. Moreover I am not quite free from self-reproach in the matter, which of all things I dread.'

The book came still-born from the press. The British public had not at any time been very much interested in the Afghan war and, now that they had Auckland's word for it that it had ended in the usual triumph, they had forgotten it. When Kabul came into the news again, nearly two years later, the book was out of date and the author had returned to his proper trade. The phrase is his own, for he wrote, 'I think that the whole affair, from beginning to end, is a pretty intelligible hint to me to stick, for the remainder of my life, to my own trade and have nothing more to do with authorship.'

CHAPTER VII

JALALABAD (1841–1842)

THE KABUL to which Havelock returned in the early months of 1841, after a journey which had lasted for half a year, was a very different place from the military station which he had left. Shah Sujah was still on his throne but no one took any interest in him. He was neither resented nor welcome, he had simply ceased to count. The true power in Kabul was that of the Politicals, to whom Auckland had given an amount of authority which enabled them to interfere with anything civil or military as the mood took them. A strong commanding general might perhaps have asserted himself, but the new commander of all troops in Afghanistan, General Elphinstone, was anything but strong. Havelock met him on his return journey at Ferozepore and travelled onwards with him, and he never tried to conceal his opinion that Elphinstone was the last man who ought to have been entrusted with such an important command at that moment.

Havelock—like everyone who knew Elphinstone—had no word to say against his courage or competence. The truth was that Elphinstone was worn out. He was an ageing man, almost totally crippled by gout, and all that he wanted was to retire. He had been urgent to be allowed to decline the appointment, knowing that he was not fit for it, but Auckland had insisted and told him that it was his duty to accept it. It was the one argument which Elphinstone had always accepted without question.

When Havelock arrived—as when he left—the main interest of the higher command was the date of their leaving Kabul. Macnaghten had been appointed Governor of Bombay and was ready to move at any time. Elphinstone had, not for the first time, sent in his resignation, and waited hopefully to hear of its acceptance. The result was a heightened interest in the lines of communication with India, where the Ghilzis were triumphantly demonstrating the profit-making capacities of private enterprise in comparison with a state subsidy. The passes of the Khyber Hills loomed large in the thoughts of the men who would soon have to attempt their passage—especially the dreaded pass of Khord Kabul, so steep and so narrow that daylight never reached the bottom of it from year's end to year's end, and where the foot-path which served for a road crossed and recrossed a stream no less than eighteen times. It was a position where a battalion of determined and well-armed men could hold up a division.

In Kabul the chief danger to the British was the situation of their cantonments. The obvious place for them to occupy was the fortification called the Bala Hissar, a strong position where they would have been practically impregnable and from which they could have dominated the city. But Shah Sujah had taken a fancy to it as a residence for his seraglio and Macnaghten had allowed him to take it, overriding Elphinstone's feeble protests. So the Army of Kabul was relegated to cantonments, which were two miles away from the centre of the city and were innocent of any but the most elementary form of protection.

There were officers in the army beside Havelock who viewed the situation with gloom and incredulous despair—Brigadier Sale, Colonel Monteith of the 35th Native Infantry, Oldfield the cavalry leader, and, above all, Havelock's old friend Major George Broadfoot. Broadfoot had served for most of his time in a Native Infantry regiment, but within the last few months he had been ordered to raise and train a company of native sappers. Had he not been comparatively junior in rank, he might have done much to save the army, for he was as sound a soldier and as honest a man as Havelock, and he had a habit of speaking his mind openly and violently without regard to the seniority of his opponent of the moment. He was the only officer in Kabul who successfully defied the Politicals and put Macnaghten in his place.

In the late summer of 1841, the Government of India, terrified by the growing cost of the occupation, decided to reduce the strength of the army at Kabul by another brigade, and Sale was ordered to take his, which included the 13th and the 35th, back to India, clearing the passes and punishing the Ghilzis on the way.

In November, the advance-guard moved out of the city and were at once attacked by strong parties of the Ghilzis, who inflicted heavy casualties on the 35th. Sale hastened to their support and they fought a running battle into and through the Khord Kabul Pass, in which Sale was badly wounded. Havelock was in action with them. He had tired of doing nothing in Kabul and had applied to Elphinstone for leave to go with the brigade as staff officer. He rode beside Sale during the battle in the Pass, in which he managed to fight with his old friends of the 13th. After the fight, when Sale decided that he could not advance without reinforcement, he asked Havelock to ride back to Kabul with his despatch and to use his influence with Elphinstone to ensure prompt and adequate support. Havelock accomplished the dangerous journey, spent a week in Kabul urging Elphinstone to action, received from Burnes the comforting assurance that there was no danger of a rising in the city, and left to rejoin Sale, whose headquarters were now at Gundamuk. Even a detached brigade was not spared the attentions of the Politicals, and a Captain Macgregor was with Sale, though he was much more reasonable and less obstructive than most of his colleagues.

Elphinstone next sent orders to Sale to establish his position at Gundamuk so as to cover the approach of the court and army when they left Kabul for their winter quarters at Jalalabad. Sale reached the town on the last day of October and set himself to carry out his instructions, and Broadfoot's sappers found plenty of employment. The Ghilzis hung round their outposts, and Akbar Khan, a vigorous and warlike son of Dost Mohammed, was in the neighbourhood with a large party of irregular horse. Sale was nearly incapacitated by his wound and, to the surprise of his officers, began to show signs of the vacillation and uncertainty which were to mark all his actions during the next months. All the army knew him as a brave soldier and a good battalion commander, but he proved to be at a loss when entrusted with an independent command, where there was no one to give him orders.

When definite news came on 10th November, it was even worse than rumour had foreshadowed. A message at last came from Elphinstone telling them of the outbreak in Kabul on the 2nd. There had been a sudden flare-up in the city, the Treasury had been sacked and several British officers had been murdered, among them Burnes and his brother and Captain William Broadfoot. But to them the incomprehensible thing was that the British appeared to have taken no action to quell or punish the revolt. And when more details trickled through, they knew that it was true, though they did not yet realise the extent of the disaster or the depths of Elphinstone's irresolution. It had begun with a mob in a street, an attack on some British houses, and soon Burnes and the other officers had been dragged out and slashed to death in the street. Shah Sujah, to do him justice, had attempted to put down the riot. Elphinstone was past all but negative action by this time and his next message to Sale's Brigade proved how desperate he was, for he ordered them to return to Kabul, if they could leave their sick in safety where they were.

Sale was in great pain from his wound and his indecision was pitiful. He summoned a council of war—a sure sign that the situation was beyond him—and laid Elphinstone's letter before them. Opinion among his officers was sharply divided, but Broadfoot and Havelock were resolute for ignoring the order. Havelock, as a junior officer without a command, had no vote in the council and had to be chary of expressing his opinion, but he spoke strongly of the impossibility of leaving 300 sick and wounded men in a defenceless position in the middle of innumerable enemies, who were known to make a practice of killing all wounded whom they found. Broadfoot, as was his manner, maintained his view with violence—so much so that Havelock, who agreed with him, spoke to him privately afterwards about his language—but his argument was sound. The brigade was eight days' march away from Kabul, and if they were to try to make their way there they might have to fight a battle on every day of the eight, though their ammunition would hold out for five days at the outside. Monteith and Oldfield were disposed to support this, though they could only give a qualified assent to Broadfoot's impassioned argument, that if Elphinstone could do nothing with 5,000 men, he was not likely to be less helpless when reinforced by one more weak brigade. Sale, Havelock commented severely, used some very regrettable language, but he could not give his officers a lead. At last the council decided that it would be useless to try to reach Kabul and wicked to endanger their wounded, and that they could best serve the army's cause by holding out where at least they kept open a way of escape should it come to that. The rightness of the decision was a matter of debate in messes and in barrack-rooms for many years afterwards. Herbert Edwardes sums up the arguments very fairly in his life of Henry Lawrence:

> 'Of course it will always remain a moot point whether Sale could have returned or not: and, if he had returned, whether he could have saved the Kabul force. From Sale's own account, it is probable that he could not have returned in a state of efficiency: but there were at least two men with Sale's Brigade who would have made all the difference—one, Henry Havelock, who would have restored the discipline of poor Elphinstone's subordinates, if mortal man could do it—the other, George Broadfoot, who in the last resort would have dared to supply the army with a leader.'

If they could not get back to Kabul—and the general opinion of later military experts is that the decision was right—it was essential that they should establish a strong position where they could hold out and at the same time cover the route which led from there to Peshawar. Havelock strongly urged the abandonment of Gundamuk in favour of Jalalabad which was a bigger place and better adapted for defence, and was tactically the best position for protecting the route. The nearest military post of any size to the east of them was Ferozepore and it was thirty-five marching days distant. Rumour said that the Afghans were hurrying towards Jalalabad hoping to occupy it and to cut the tenuous line of communication on which the Army of Kabul depended. Sale and the other senior officers had recognised by this time that Havelock's advice on a tactical problem was not to be lightly disregarded and they prepared for a move before the enemy could forestall them. As it was, they had to fight their way against constant attacks and their march for much of the way was overlooked by heights on which the enemy swarmed, harassing them with long-range fire from their Jezail muskets. They had to pass through the little town of Futtehabad on their route and outside it the Afghans, becoming more venturesome, attacked them in the open plain, but were held off by Broadfoot's sappers, who formed the rearguard that day, and were then dispersed with some loss by Oldfield's cavalry. They won through to Jalalabad and at once began to put it into a state of defence.

It was no light task, as the despatch which Havelock wrote for Sale did not hesitate to explain:

> 'The walls were in a state which might have justified despair as to the possibility of defending them. The enceinte was far too extensive for our small force, embracing a circumference of more than 2,500 yards. It had no parapet, except for a few hundred yards, while there was not more than two feet high of earth. . . . There was a space of 400 yards on which none of the garrison could show themselves excepting at one spot. The population was disaffected and the whole enceinte was surrounded by ruined forts, walls, mosques, tombs and gardens.'

The brigade had hardly entered the town before the Afghans began to harass them, and it seemed likely that they would try to mount an assault before the defences could be manned and put into order. Havelock calculated that, by the end of the first day of occupation, there were not less than five thousand enemy surrounding the city. At first the walls were so bad that the enemy penetrated them and set fire to some buildings in the outer districts, though, on the whole, this was to the advantage of the defenders, as it cleared a field of fire for them and destroyed some of the cover which might have helped an assaulting force.

The brigade had entered on 12th November and, two days later, Sale determined to strike a blow to make the enemy more careful in their approach. Monteith commanded a sortie of 1,100 of all arms and drove the enemy away, inflicting some casualties, including 200 killed. It was a salutary lesson and the Afghans learned from it. For a long time afterwards they confined their efforts to harassing tactics and long-range sniping.

The chief anxiety of the garrison was not shortage of food or even of ammunition but of news from their comrades in Kabul. Soon after they had occupied the city, Sale had received a letter from Elphinstone, which implored him, almost abjectly, to break out and come to his help. There was no need for a council of war to discuss it. The garrison could not have broken out if they had wanted to.

The next news was so unforeseen, so disastrous, that at first the garrison could not bring themselves to believe it. That Macnaghten might have been murdered and that the army in Kabul might be in trouble, they could credit, but they indignantly rejected the story that 5,000 British troops had laid down their arms and capitulated. But every day which followed strengthened the tale and added new details. A proclamation issued by Akbar Khan, found its way into the town and announced that the whole country had risen against the hated Feringhees, that many of them had been killed inside Kabul, and that the whole army had perished in trying to make their escape through the mountains. Still the garrison hoped against declining hope, knowing that any proclamation of the enemy would be exaggerated if not wholly untrue, but on 9th January, 1842, an official despatch signed by Elphinstone and dated 2nd December tore away the last shreds of that hope.

Three Afghans, men of authority, entered the town under flag of truce and delivered the despatch and Sale gathered his senior officers together to hear it. None of them ever forgot the shame of that day. Elphinstone wrote that Macnaghten had been treacherously murdered and that, since he could no longer supply his troops or hope to break out, he had capitulated with his whole army. He ordered the garrison of Jalalabad to abandon their position and retreat to Peshawar, leaving their guns in position in the citadel, together with all stores and baggage which they could not carry with them. The surrender of Jalalabad had been included in the terms of the capitulation and Elphinstone added —a piece of credulous imbecility of which even he could hardly have been suspected—'Everything has been done in good faith; you will not be molested on your way; and to the safe conduct which Akbar

Khan has given I trust for the passage of the troops under my command.'

Anyone who trusted in Akbar was lost indeed and, only three days later, the garrison had proof of it. Havelock was one of a group of officers who stood on a roof-top in Jalalabad and saw the arrival of the only survivor of the army of Kabul.

> 'About 2 p.m. [he wrote], on the 13th January, some officers were assembled on the roof of the loftiest house in Jalalabad. One of them espied a single horseman riding towards our walls. As he got nearer, it was distinctly seen that he wore European clothing and was mounted on a travel-backed yaboo, which he was urging on with all the speed of which it yet remained master. A signal was made to him from someone on the walls, which he answered by waving a private soldier's forage cap over his head. The Kabul Gate was thrown open and several officers, rushing out, received and recognised in the traveller, who dismounted, the first, and it is to be feared, the last fugitive of the ill-fated force at Kabul, in Dr. Brydon. He was covered with slight cuts and contusions and dreadfully exhausted. His first few hasty sentences extinguished all hope in the hearts of the listeners regarding the fortune of the Kabul force. It was evident that it was annihilated.'

The story was so terrible, the destruction so complete, that though they heard it from one who had survived it, they could not bring themselves to believe that it was the end of an army—that no belated and wounded survivors would come limping towards the town where the British flag flew to welcome and protect them. Oldfield's cavalry saddled and rode through the gates to patrol the surrounding country-side, only to return without result or hope when at last night fell. All that night and for three nights afterwards a beacon burned on the walls, and buglers in relays of four at a time sounded the 'Advance' every half-hour. An officer whose quarters were in the Citadel remarked that the wind was in the adverse quarter and that the notes of the bugles were blown backwards to sound like a dirge over the roofs of the town.

But the Army of Kabul was lying dead in the snow among the passes of the Khyber Hills. Elphinstone had marched out with over 5,000 troops and 12,000 camp-followers—civilians among whom were many women and children. The Ghilzis had fallen on them and Akbar Khan had betrayed them. The long agony went on through the winter nights and days, by rifle-fire, by the knife, by death from frost and exposure. There were many incidents of gallantry by the British troops who formed the rear-guard, but the Khord Kabul Pass, where the narrow road was blocked and the riflemen waited for them, put an end to them as an organised army, and turned them into a huddle of driven sheep, without food or ammunition, with limbs so frozen that they could hardly stand or walk and their hands could no longer grip their muskets; dropping by hundreds, as the Afghans cut down the British and stripped the native camp-followers naked and left them to die in the cold; till at the end of their *via dolorosa* there was only a small party of the rear-guard of the 44th Foot: then only three subalterns who had fought it out beside their men till all were killed and had managed to escape for a few miles further till their horses foundered, and Dr. Brydon stumbled on alone to bring the news to Jalalabad.

For the garrison there the question remained as to what action they should take in view of the orders which they had received to capitulate. There could be little hesitation since, as far as they knew, Elphinstone was dead and his orders no longer valid. They held themselves bound to hold on to what was, for all they knew, the last vestige of British power in Afghanistan. They hoped of course for relief from India, where troops were already being despatched to Peshawar to make up the relieving columns, but they could not expect much from this source for some time. Colonel Wilde had started from Peshawar already but news, which had come from him during the previous twenty-four hours, told them that his attempt had failed. General Pollock had just arrived in Peshawar but he had at the moment only two battalions under his hand. Sale had estimated that the minimum necessary for a relieving force would be 6,000 men. The garrison knew that Pollock would not delay a moment longer than was necessary and that there would be nothing half-hearted about any attempt which he would make, but the question was whether they could hold out until his arrival. They had food enough for three months, on half-rations, but there was a much more serious shortage of ammunition, nor had they any big guns should the Afghans mount a real attack in force on the walls. Havelock noted that their chief needs were for 'eight 18-pounders, four mortars and'—a characteristic addition—'a chaplain. . . .'

> 'The heart of the Garrison [he wrote] is good, and we are ready, with God's help for a manful struggle, if the Government will support us with vigour. We are ready to fight either in open field, or behind our walls, or both. But in March we shall have famine staring us in the face, and probably disease assailing us. Our position is therefore most critical: but there is not I trust, an ounce of despondency among us.'

They were brave words and he believed them for his trust in God was a very real thing, but if he were not despondent, others were and among them was Sale, the commandant of the garrison. Sale's wound had not healed, he was weak and often in pain, and his courage, which had never failed in battle, was not of the sort to stand the strain of such responsibility. Several of the senior officers were inclined to agree with him that Elphinstone's orders and subsequent defeat would justify them in making the best terms which they could for their own escape. On 26th January a letter from the court of Shah Sujah was brought into the town, telling them that a treaty was in existence which bound all the British to leave Afghanistan and setting out the terms on which they were to capitulate. Shah Sujah had added a private note addressed to the resident Political officer in Jalalabad, Macgregor, explaining that he was in the hands of the extremists among his own subjects, but would do what he could to help the garrison out of their predicament. Sale apparently agreed with Macgregor in attaching some value to this offer. Broadfoot and Havelock regarded it with contempt and incredulity. Sale, as was his habit, summoned a council of war, to help him to make up his mind. It lasted for two days and was afterwards referred to by Havelock as 'The Jackdaw's Parliament'.

In the first day's debate the general feeling was in favour of trying to make terms with Shah Sujah, and almost the only opposition was provided by Broadfoot and Havelock. Havelock was handicapped by not having a vote or the right to speak except by courtesy of his seniors, but he loyally supported Broadfoot, who led the opposition with his usual force—in fact with so much that Havelock feared that his violence of speech did harm to his cause and aroused disagreement in the others. Broadfoot related afterwards how Havelock had sat with him in his quarters far into that night pleading for a more reasoned and less passionate appeal to the council. At the end of the day's proceedings Sale had lost all patience with Broadfoot, and the debate had ended in tumult.

They met again next morning to discuss the enemy's terms, and Broadfoot schooled himself to moderation. The terms were such as to give pause to officers who had argued in favour of capitulation on principle. The garrison were to march out at once, leaving behind them all their guns and any stores which they could not carry with them. They were to be given safe-conduct as far as Peshawar and to exchange hostages with the enemy, which were to be restored on arrival at Peshawar.

The question of hostages and safe-conduct prevented acceptance of the terms even by those who had supported the principle. They could not forget that the Kabul army had also had Akbar Khan's guarantee of a safe journey, and most of them flatly refused to consider any giving of hostages. Oldfield, who had been undecided the day before, suddenly flared into anger and swung round to the support of the opposition. 'I for one', he said hotly, 'will fight here to the last drop of my blood, but I plainly declare that I will never be a hostage and I am surprised anyone should propose such a thing, or think that an Afghan's word is to be relied on.' Broadfoot followed him with a return of his earlier vehemence. 'So long as we are an army, I obey orders: but once we capitulate, the first shot which violates the capitulation sets me free to act as I please.' Colonel Monteith was moved to quote poetry, causing Havelock to record later: 'The fact of the gallant colonel's usual declamation being something of the character of prose on stilts might have prevented me from remarking that he had taken a flight into the poetic region.'

At the end of it all they played for time, sending messages back to ask for more detailed information about the hostage arrangement. Time was their one hope, for any day now Pollock would be on the march and, though it must take him many weeks to force the passes and cross the plain, their troops would fight with renewed energy if they knew that help was on the way. The men were heartened a few days later by a successful raid into the surrounding country in which their whole force of cavalry and the sappers rounded up 170 cattle and over 700 sheep and drove them into the town. The Afghan cavalry, who followed them too late, were astonished to find the walls crowned with capering soldiers imitating the baa-ing of sheep for their benefit.

In February Shah Sujah answered their letter with a request that, if they really meant to treat, the principal officers should affix their seals to the terms of capitulation, but, though Sale and Macgregor were for complying, the others had been won over by Broadfoot and Havelock, and the garrison sent an unfavourable reply. They were in touch with Pollock in Peshawar and he encouraged them, though he could give them no good news about an early arrival, since he was experiencing the greatest difficulty in assembling a force and was quite without cavalry. He doubted now whether he would be able to leave Peshawar before the end of April: and the middle of the month was the date by which their provisions would be exhausted.

At Jalalabad the days dragged on, the stocks of food and ammunition drained away, and, for further discouragement, a violent earth-tremor on 19th February almost completely destroyed their painfully built walls. The Afghans were all round the town, since Akbar Khan's cavalry had joined the investing forces, but still they would not risk an assault. The whole garrison slaved at repairing the damage and for a month their life was a nightmare of days with pick and shovel, nights of guard duty and constant alarms and assemblies to beat off a threatened attack on some weak point of the enceinte. Shah Sujah had given them another chance of capitulating, which they had answered with the crushing request that he should address himself to General Pollock at Peshawar, the commander of H.M.'s troops in Afghanistan. Havelock was right in saying that the heart of the garrison was good and that there was no despondency, but most of the senior officers knew that their chance of holding out till Pollock's coming was a slight one and that any mischance would wipe it out altogether. Havelock discussed their chances with Broadfoot and with Oldfield and Monteith, and at last they came to the decision that, if the siege were ever to be raised, they must raise it themselves. Their plan was for an all-out attack on the enemy in the open, to be delivered by the whole available strength of the garrison.

Havelock was given the task of persuading Sale that in such an attack lay their sole chance of deliverance. Sale at first refused to listen, but all the senior officers went to him in a body and urged the necessity of the plan, and at last he gave in.

Havelock wrote the orders for the battle and the date was fixed for 7th April. Akbar's strength was estimated at about 6,000 and the British attacked in three columns, not one of which was of more than 500 men, with the support of a field-battery and such few cavalry as still had horses fit for the work. Broadfoot had been badly wounded in a sortie a few days earlier and could not take part in it, and Havelock took over command of the right column, which should have been his. This wing, only 360 strong, had to beat off the fiercest of the Afghan counter-attacks, when Akbar launched 1,500 of his horsemen in a charge on them. The British formed square and Akbar's horsemen went down before their musketry as Ney's squadrons had gone down at Waterloo. They nearly lost their commander, for Havelock was outside the square, directing its formation when the cavalry came on, and he only just managed to get back in time. Sale, who was as courageous in battle as he was timid in council, led the centre which met stiff opposition from a ruined fort which was held in unexpected strength. It was all over by 7 p.m. and the Afghans were in flight over the plain, leaving hundreds of dead behind them. The siege of Jalalabad, which had lasted for five months, was over. There can be few instances in military history of a garrison which has been besieged for so long and has finally extricated itself by attacking its besiegers. A week later, when Pollock's advance-guard marched into the town, they were greeted by the band of the 13th with the old Scots air, 'O, but you've been lang in coming.'

CHAPTER

VIII

THE FORTY-EIGHT HOURS WAR (1842–1843)

THERE WAS a new government in England in the year 1842 and a new Governor-General in India, where Lord Ellenborough arrived in March to replace Lord Auckland. As soon as Ellenborough landed he published a spirited statement declaring the government's intention of re-establishing the British military power in Afghanistan and teaching its people a lesson. The preparations for this strong action lagged somewhat behind the intention and Pollock's men and the Jalalabad garrison were left to kick their heels till August, when the concerted march on Kabul was due to begin. There was a new C.-in-C. India too. Sir Jasper Nicholls had retired after a short tenure and had been replaced by Sir Hugh Gough, fresh from his triumphs in China.

For the present, Havelock found time hang heavy on his hands and his thoughts turned inevitably to his old worry about finance and his family. His wife and children had been on leave in England during the war in Afghanistan, but they were now on the way out again and he must find some means of providing for them. He had had twenty-eight years' service and was still no more than a captain, and he began anxiously to write to his friends about his chances of employment or promotion. By painful means of economy he had been able to save enough to purchase his majority if he could find a seller at the standard price. So desperate was he that he even thought of abjuring his resolve to give up authorship and of bringing up to date his Afghanistan history, ill-fated though the early volumes had been. Broadfoot dissuaded him with his usual common sense and outspokenness, telling him that if he omitted the worst part of the story his book would be a failure and if he told it all, he would lose his commission. Sale, who was always a good friend, knew of his plight and generously wrote to Pollock asking for employment for him as an interpreter. Pollock was willing, but before it was settled Havelock was offered and accepted the post of Deputy Adjutant-General on the staff of McGaskill's division which was to be part of the force in Afghanistan in the new campaign.

Once again a British army passed through the Khord Kabul pass, marching through the relics of the army which had perished there. Their passage was opposed, but this time they were strong, well equipped and, most important of all, well led. Broadfoot's Ghurkas scrambled over the heights and chased and destroyed the astonished Afghans who had thought themselves impregnable there and were dismayed by these little men who climbed like goats and fought like tigers. The whole British Army were burning for revenge and they made a terrible slaughter at Tezin, driving Akbar Khan and his men before them, and making a triumphant entry into Kabul. The enemy had fled before them but had rallied in the Kohistan, and McGaskill's division were sent out to make an end of them. McGaskill had a high opinion of Havelock's military skill—and a pleasantly modest one of his own—and appointed him to command the division in the action. Havelock's battle order shows how carefully he thought out his movements and how little reliance he placed on the frontal attack which formed the basis of most British tactics at the time. His division enveloped the enemy and inflicted drastic punishment on them. One of the political officers, who had been captured in Kabul and had been released by the relieving force, Major Pottinger, said to him after the fight, 'Oh, if only we had had you with us at Kabul, things would have worn a very different aspect.' Havelock's modest reply was, 'I will not undertake to say that I could have saved Kabul; but I feel confident that George Broadfoot could have done it.'

Britain's prestige had been restored and her military honour vindicated, but the war had been terribly expensive and the Government turned to thoughts of economy. The first thing to do, of course, was to withdraw the army from Kabul and to break it up, so that it could return to its normal duties and so that extravagant luxuries like staff-captains would no longer be needed. The immediate effect on Havelock was to reduce the total of his pay and allowances by exactly half.

He was consoled for this by the award of the companionship of the Order of the Bath, which brought him no financial advantage, but he was no nearer to promotion. Havelock wrote despondently to his old friend General Harry Smith, since all that was in prospect for him was a return to regimental employment as a company commander. He wrote rather pathetically:

'Now in a word, I will tell you what I want. I desire not to have to starve on 400 rupees a month when I return to the provinces, and to have some better employment than looking at the shirts and the stockings of No. 4 Coy. of the 13th, though they *did* pitch it into Akbar Khan's horse in such good style in the hour of need.'

Smith had nothing to offer him, nor could his influence be of much help for, good soldier though he was, his habit of openly criticising his superiors did not add to his popularity. So Havelock returned a little disconsolately to his regiment and to his company's shirts and stockings. His wife and children had arrived in India and soon he was able to take them to Simla for a long leave. At the moment it seemed that he might be able to purchase his next step, since one of the majors in the 13th was talking about selling out and the money for purchase was lying in the bank at Calcutta. Once again the prospect faded to nothing, yet once again it was lucky for him, because he got the step without paying for it at the end of the year, when another major retired unexpectedly. By a further piece of luck, the new Governor-General, Lord Ellenborough, went on a long tour of the upper provinces and his place at the head of the Government was temporarily filled by the senior member of the Council, Mr. Wilberforce Bird, who happened to be a friend of the Marshman family. Sir Hugh Gough had just arrived to take over the duties of Commander-in-Chief and Mr. Bird appointed Havelock to his staff as interpreter in Persian. It was a subordinate position, but it brought him into touch with the Headquarters of the Army in India and with Gough, who became and always remained a good friend and staunch supporter. Havelock had the satisfaction of knowing that, if war should break out at any time—and the Army in India was seldom inactive for long—he was in a position favourable for attracting notice when trained staff-officers were needed. They were needed, only eight months after his appointment, for the Gwalior campaign, which came to be known as the Forty-eight Hours War. The trouble in the state of Gwalior began, as was common in India, with a dispute about the succession to a throne and the consequent anxiety in British minds about the new ruler's attitude towards the Raj. It was soon plain that the policy of the new régime in Gwalior was anti-European, and especially anti-British. The Dada Sahib at once dismissed all the European officers from his forces, though they were responsible for their high efficiency.

Colonel Spiers, the British Resident, was convinced that this was only the beginning of unfriendly actions against his country and reported his fears to Ellenborough, who, in reply, wrote rather ominously, that

'He hoped that there might be no outrage which would render necessary the bringing together of troops for the vindication of the British Government.' At the same time he proved how vain was his hope by ordering the establishment of a 'Camp of Exercise' at Agra, which was within easy reach of the Gwalior frontier. It was a flimsy and, by this time, almost formal pretext for preparing for war.

The troops assembled during the summer of 1843 and, when Gough had arrived in Bengal, Ellenborough wrote to him:

> 'You can have but little rest in Calcutta, for the state of affairs in Gwalior makes it necessary that your own camp should be formed in Cawnpore on the 15th of October and a large camp of exercise and observation (if not for operations in the field), in the vicinity of Agra by the first of November.'

There did not seem to be any immediate danger of an attack from inside the Gwalior border, but the Governor-General could hardly be satisfied while an army of such strength, without European officers, remained as a permanent threat. He insisted on a drastic reduction in its numbers and, since the ruler of Gwalior made no attempt to comply, he ordered Gough to cross the border and enforce his decree. On 22nd December Gough and his army crossed the border, expecting to meet with no resistance, since Ellenborough had remarked that it would be 'nothing but a military parade'. Gough was so far in agreement that he invited the Governor-General and Lady Ellenborough, who had come with other ladies to see the 'parade', to dinner on Christmas day in the capital of Gwalior.

Gough was a great fighter but an indifferent tactician and his force crossed the border at several points, far enough apart to make it impossible for any of them to move quickly to the support of any other. In a few hours the left wing met with resistance at Punniar, but the enemy were not strong and General Grey's division drove them off without difficulty. Gough, with the right wing, marched straight on and met the bulk of the enemy near Maharahjpore, late in the afternoon of 18th December.

After a perfunctory reconnaissance they camped for the night. During it, the enemy, for what reason it is difficult to imagine, abandoned their strong position and took up one much less defensible a few miles away, with the result that when next day Gough, disdaining further reconnaissance, moved boldly forward, his army were under heavy fire before they knew that they had reached the enemy. The first that the spectators, who included Lady Ellenborough, Lady and Miss

Gough, Mrs. Harry Smith and a Mrs. Curtis, knew of it was a cannon-shot which took off the ear of one of the elephants on which they were mounted. The elephants turned and ran, and Gough, casting aside with relief the duty of manœuvring, turned joyfully to the congenial task of fighting. It was always his habit to wear a white coat in battle, so that the troops might see him clearly and be encouraged, and he went into the thick of it with Havelock beside him. Once one of the regiments of native infantry showed reluctance to face the fire of the guns and Havelock galloped across to them, rallied them and led them into action. It was a hard fight, destitute of tactics or manœuvre, a struggle with rifle and bayonet and the casualties on both sides were heavy, the British losing over a thousand in killed and wounded. Havelock never made any comment on it afterwards, though he was unjustly accused of having written some articles which appeared in one of the papers and freely condemned Gough's headlong methods. He was not to be drawn into controversy. As he wrote to a friend, 'Seeing a disposition to identify me with any remarks on military matters you might publish, I felt obliged to apply to myself till the storm had blown over, the advice of Matthew Prior's stroller:

> '*Mind neither good nor bad nor right nor wrong,*
> *But eat thy pudding, slave, and hold thy tongue.*'

It was at any rate a decisive victory for the British and the campaign closed with the battle. Ellenborough was able to impose his reduction on the army at Gwalior and substituted a force under British officers. Among the native officers who were trained in it was a promising young soldier called Tantia Topee, whom Havelock was to meet again outside Cawnpore fourteen years later.

It cannot be said that the campaign had taught Havelock very much —at least in a positive way—but it helped his fortunes, in that Gough, who was as generous as he was brave and who admired bravery in other men as unfailingly as he practised it himself, noticed his staff officer's cool courage under fire and resolved to keep so good a soldier with him. So when the force was disbanded to return to its home stations and Gough went off on a tour of the North-Western districts, Havelock accompanied him. After thirty years' service, he was a lieutenant-colonel by brevet.

CHAPTER IX

THE SIKH WAR (1845–1846)

THE GWALIOR campaign had hardly ended when there were signs that another storm was blowing up, this time among the Sikhs, now that death had removed the strong arm and stout heart of Ranjit Singh. Broadfoot had recently been appointed Resident at Lahore and was sending disturbing reports about the situation there. There had been the usual trouble about succession to the throne and, as a result, the real power in the country was the Khalsa, the Sikh army. It was a strong and efficient force, for the Sikhs were a fighting race and their troops had been trained and organised by French officers, under an able soldier, General Avitabile.

Ellenborough had gone home and had been succeeded by Sir Henry Hardinge, a Peninsular veteran, who had barely taken over his new duties when the Khalsa broke out in revolt. Gough hastened to meet them with as strong a force as he could collect and with a staff on which both Havelock and his old friend, Broadfoot, served, while the Quartermaster-General was another old friend, Sir Robert Sale. Hardinge had not heard a shot fired for thirty years, but he smelt powder and came posting across India to join the army at its point of assembly. On 28th December, Gough's advance-guard were at Mudki, about 10,000 strong, when they learned that the Sikhs with about 12,000 of all arms and twenty-two guns were advancing to meet them. The two armies met head-on at Mudki and the battle which followed was without manœuvre or tactics and just such a hand-to-hand infantry fight as Gough loved. For all its ferocity, the fight was short. The armies had met about four o'clock in the afternoon and before darkness fell the Sikh cavalry had galloped away, leaving their infantry to fend for themselves. Night and the thick jungle behind the battlefield saved them, since they could not be pursued. The British losses were 257 killed and 657 wounded.

During much of the fighting Havelock and Broadfoot rode side by side, and when Havelock's favourite charger, 'Feroze', was struck by a round-shot and fell, crushing his master beneath him, Broadfoot dragged him out and found him another horse. In a few minutes man and horse were down again and Broadfoot, throwing him up into a third saddle, remarked that it was a waste of horseflesh to mount him, as he was sure to lose them all.

The British rested for two days and then advanced and came upon the enemy on 21st December at Ferozeshah. Once again it was late in the day and Gough was afterwards criticised for his decision to attack at once, when so few hours of daylight were left. Havelock always defended the decision. He considered it, he wrote, 'of the last consequence to strike a blow at the Ferozeshah force in the full confidence of success, before it could be reinforced by the army blockading Ferozephore. . . . It was one of those cases when it would have been better to attack at midnight, rather than not to have anticipated the junction of the two armies. . . . The resistance', he added, 'was terrific and the loss on our side tremendous—but this is War.' The Sikhs were strongly entrenched and, for the first time, the British found themselves facing the full weight of the Sikh artillery against which their own guns, fewer in number and much lighter in metal, could make no headway. Once again it was the British infantry who had to do the work, though the 3rd Dragoons made another charge such as had won the name of the Mudki-wallahs in their last fight. Daylight failed before the battle was over and both sides slept on the field of battle, with the chances of victory still even. Again the British losses were heavy—they were seldom light when Gough commanded—amounting to 694 killed and 1,721 wounded, of whom nearly three-quarters were Queen's troops. The 3rd Dragoons alone, who had been sent against entrenched artillery, lost in two days' fighting over two hundred men and a hundred horses. Among the British dead were both Broadfoot and Sale.

At the end of the second day's fighting the Sikhs were glad to break off when darkness came again and to escape once more from pursuit, of which the British were hardly capable had there been light enough for it. There was an uneasy interlude after that of nearly a month while the exhausted armies rested and renewed their strength, though this favoured the Sikhs, who were easily reinforced from Lahore, and not the British whose reinforcements had a long way to come. Fighting began again on 28th January, 1846, when a small Sikh force was defeated by a division commanded by Sir Harry Smith, who, as

Captain Smith, had been Havelock's company commander at Shorncliffe, more than twenty years earlier. On 10th February the full armies clashed at Sobraon.

Sobraon was an even deadlier form of the two earlier battles, with the Sikhs entrenched and the British committed to a frontal attack, and with an even greater weight of Sikh artillery. At first the British could make no progress and their centre was nearly destroyed by the heavy guns, but the divisions on the right and left pushed on until they succeeded in penetrating into the Sikh position. The fight went on through the entrenched camp and slowly the Sikhs were forced back upon the river which flowed behind it. Their bridge of boats gave way as the first fugitives tried to cross it, and the British horse artillery galloped up and blew the rest of it into matchwood. The Sikhs turned at bay on the bank and the British cavalary swept into and over them, while the riflemen stood on the bank and shot hundreds of those who tried to swim to safety. The British had learned how, after the last battles, the Sikhs had butchered the wounded, and they spared none whom they could kill. When it was over the Khalsa had ceased to exist as an army, but it was at a terrible price in British lives. The total casualties were 320 killed and 2,063 wounded, and this time the Company's native troops had suffered almost as heavily as the Queen's. As Havelock wearily dismounted at the end of the day he said to a friend, 'I thought I knew something about war. Now I see that I knew nothing till today.'

CHAPTER

X

ENGLAND (1847–1851)

HAVELOCK WAS over fifty now, and, though he was a lieutenant-colonel by brevet, his substantive rank and pay were those of major. Moreover, his appointment on Gough's staff ended with the end of the Sikh campaign, and, unless something else were soon to be forthcoming, he had no prospect better than a return to the shirts and stockings. He had the money for his next step, but the senior officers of the 13th seemed to be immortal, and, very reluctantly, he exchanged into the 39th, where the prospects seemed a little brighter. Fortunately Lord Hardinge, on his own responsibility, had decided that so efficient a staff-officer and so brave a man ought to be kept in staff employment, and wrote personally to the Duke of Wellington on his behalf. The Duke was ready to help and appointed him Deputy Adjutant-General of The Queen's Troops in Bengal, where he found himself once more under his old chief, Sir Willoughby Cotton.

The strain of constant service in the field had told on his strength, and, before he had been for three months in his new appointment, he was invalided with another bad attack of 'intermittent fever'. 'The fact is', he wrote, 'my constitution has been insensibly but deeply undermined by eight years' heavy and harassing work.' He further complained bitterly of the effect on his liver of residence at a Command Headquarters, with the high living which was in those days an inseparable part of life there. 'I have passed from the most ascetic habits to feasting with rulers, and from cold water and three fasts in the week, to washing down pomfret and iced delicacies with champagne and golden sherry.' He had allowed himself a little indulgence on the advice of his doctors, who firmly believed that a course of cold water was enough to ruin the health of any reasonable man, though he himself attributed the return of his old trouble, at least in part, to some foul water which he had drunk during the late campaign. 'The sense of thirst was intolerable. . . . It is now plain that, whatever the cause, my liver has been much affected, and that the genuine and strong drink, though administered quite secundum artem, was so much poison.' He was low enough in body and spirit to write to Marshman, 'I have felt during some portions of this sickness, a longing for a Christian's rest, relying on the Christian's hope: but the sight and the thought of my unprotected wife and children makes me wish for life, though with labour and vexation until their lot is more settled.'

Hannah, too, was ailing though the children were in good health, and Havelock began to explore the possibilities of their all returning to England. As was always his misfortune, expense was the obstacle.

> 'As for the means of going [he wrote], difficulties accumulate around me every day. I shall not be out of the hands of the Simla Jews before February next. The expense of living and marching here, though conducted with the utmost economy, are necessarily heavy: and Harry and Joshua have to be maintained and educated. . . . So that if it were not for an over-ruling Providence to untie knots, it would be Macbeth's case,
>
> *There is no flying hence, nor tarrying here.*'

He was beginning to be appalled at the cost of living in the style which Headquarters seemed to require, though he made frantic attempts to reduce his own expenditure as far as he could. 'I have backed out of every expense that can be spared'. Another letters says:

> 'See no company and never dine even with a secretary, with no-one, in short, but the Commander-in-Chief or the Governor. But my unavoidable expenses are heavy. Horses, uniform, houses at three several places eat up money awfully, and then supervene education bills. . . .'

He had almost made up his mind by March 1848 that he must return to England, whatever the cost, if his health were ever to improve, but at the last moment the thought of his wife and family held him back. If he were to die in India, while still serving in his present rank, all that would be left for his family would be his Major's pension of £70 a year and his capital which amounted to barely £1,000. The Queen's Widow's Fund would provide them with a free passage home, but after that the country and the Army would have finished with them. His doctors were insistent that he ought to go home for at least a year, but as he said, 'There my sixteen shillings pay per diem will give us bread and salt but would not give my boy education, or my girls instruction of a tolerable kind.' In April he decided that he could not afford to leave his appointment and would have to serve abroad, for at any rate some time longer. Luckily his health had begun to improve —perhaps now that he had taken a final decision, his mind was more at ease—and the doctors told him that he could spend another year out in India without undue risk. Much might happen in a year, and, since the 39th Foot had offered no speedier promotion than his old regiment, he made one more exchange, this time into the 53rd.

He never did duty with either of these regiments. They were only moves in his ceaseless quest for security as represented by promotion and substantive rank. He could pay his way as long as he could be sure of a succession of staff appointments, but it was an anxious business. He knew the Army well enough to be assured that any day there might be a change in the Higher Command, bringing with it new Generals with their own protégés, sometimes their own friends or relations, to be provided for. But his thoughts were soon to be distracted from his own worries by the outbreak of another Sikh war. At the beginning of 1848, Lord Hardinge had returned to England after announcing that such a state of Peace prevailed in India that 'not another shot would be fired there for seven years'. Before the end of the year his prophecy was disproved, the British and the Sikhs were at each other's throats again, and Sir Hugh Gough was preparing to renew the tactics which had proved so successful only four years earlier. In November Havelock learned that his brother, William, had been killed, leading his regiment, the 14th Light Dragoons, in a cavalry charge at Ramnuggur.

William's death was a bitter blow to his brother. Henry was a soldier and had faced danger and death in action, and he knew that such were the common chances of his fellows and himself. The bitterness lay in the fact that his brother had died in a charge which should never have been ordered at all, least of all in such a casual and careless way. The C.-in-C. had blundered badly, and his impetuous and haphazard way of giving orders had cost the lives of a cavalry Brigadier and of the Commanding Officer and many of the men and horses of a regiment. And, perhaps worst of all, it was being freely said that William Havelock's own rashness had been the sole cause of the destruction. His brother Henry defended him hotly in a letter addressed to an old friend, Colonel Birch, Judge-Advocate-General of the Bengal Army.

> 'As regards the operation, it must be clear to any unprejudiced person that it ought never to have been undertaken. You may remember our pickets being driven in some weeks before the affair at Sobraon: it was the commencement of the enemy's attempt to establish himself on the left bank. The reason which I gave then against attempting counter-manœuvres

is perfectly applicable to the case of the Chenab. The enemy had a powerful artillery on the right bank, and, until its fire could be subdued, were fairly to be considered the proprietors of the stream, and of as much ground beyond it as could be swept by the fire of their guns. Their horse, pushed forward on the left bank, were intended to bravado and decoy, and should have been simply left alone, or cannonaded when convenient and possible, by guns out of reach of those of the enemy. . . . I see that you, and possibly others, have formed the opinion that my brother's impetuosity led him further than it should have done. It may have been so. Old Will was a fox-hunter before he was a soldier, and has been a hog-hunter since. . . . But his proposal should have been negatived at once, if not according to military rule, which it was clear it was not. Whether he went too far or not, and whether the scheme of the attack originated with him or not, are minor questions. The Commander-in-Chief and the General of Division were both in the field, and, as I believe, on the spot. Neither the public nor posterity will consent to fix the responsibility on any shoulders but those of the seniors: it is the irreversible decree of military history that there it must rest, and history will have it so.'

Worse was to follow. In January 1849 Gough blundered into the enemy again and, on the 13th, fought the desperate and disastrous battle of Chillianwalia. Havelock calls it 'one of the most sanguinary ever fought by the British in India and the nearest approximation to a defeat of any of the great conflicts of that power in the East'. The British claimed it as a victory and it is true that the enemy retired and left them in possession of the field but they had only gone back for three miles, and, though badly mauled, were ready to fight again. The British cavalry were ill-led and a confusion in their orders led to a panic, so that the infantry saw the unbelievable sight of their cavalry flying in disorder to the rear, with a comparatively small body of enemy horse in pursuit—and not only running away, but, in their panic, riding through and overturning their own guns and creating havoc in the waggon-lines. The British casualties in the battle were 89 officers and 2,357 other ranks.

The Government hailed it as a great victory and the bells were rung and the guns roared in salute, but they could not drown the swelling chorus of disgust and reprobation at so costly and so barren a victory. The Indian Press were unanimous in condemning the strategy and tactics of the battle and in England there was a storm of indignation which swept away the foolish attempt to cover up the loss and the shame. British guns had been lost, British standards taken and British cavalry had run like rats from the enemy. The critics won the day and the Government decided to recall Gough, but, before their order had reached him he had won another victory at Gujerat on 21st February and finished the campaign.

In the same month the 53rd Foot had been ordered to join Gough's army, and Havelock had got Cotton's leave to accompany them. It was nominally his regiment at the moment and he felt that he could not afford to miss any chance of active service. But early in March he was peremptorily recalled to Calcutta, where he received a reprimand for leaving his post at Headquarters. Cotton, whose fault it was, was also rebuked for releasing an officer for duty without the C.-in-C.'s permission. The official explanation of this rebuff to both of them was that Havelock's rank would make it impossible to employ him in a suitable post without altering the arrangements of the C.-in-C. As a brevet lieutenant-colonel on the staff, he could not be assigned to anything less than a brigade and there were no brigades without a commander. As he said himself, 'I am not wanted as a major and shall not be appointed as a Brigadier.'

He felt himself to blame, because there had been some informality in the arrangement between Cotton and himself and the C.-in-C.'s permission had apparently been taken for granted. This was, for a time, a source of some anxiety to him, since such a reprimand, if reported to the Horse Guards, could not fail to have a bad effect on his future career. With his usual honesty, he examined his share of the responsibility in a letter to his brother-in-law.

> 'I have no cause to arraign Lord Gough's conduct in ordering me back to Bombay. I have coolly weighed the matter, and, as I never like to lie myself out of scrapes, I freely confess the fault has been my own. The fact is that I allowed my mind to be biased on the subject of the 53rd going on service without me, and acted wrong, though under the strongest sense of duty. On hearing the first report of my regiment being ordered forward to Lahore, I ought to have simply written to Sir Willoughby, for Lord Gough's permission, to join it. All this I see clearly now, but what is the use of after wisdom? Neither Sir Willoughby nor I saw it at the time. My pecuniary loss will be most heavy, and my position deteriorated as, besides the loss of reputation attending every error, I have got a reprimand, and shall get another from the Horse Guards. The latter might displace me, but I do not think they will carry matters so far, the error being on the side of fight.'

His anxiety was unnecessary and he heard no more of the matter. If the report of his reprimand ever reached the Horse Guards, they ignored it—or more probably filed and forgot it—and Gough had trouble of his own to occupy his attention. The news of his recall reached him soon after his triumph at Gujerat and it was a bitterly disappointed and resentful man who returned to England. The army were genuinely sorry to see him go. Whatever his shortcomings as a tactician had been, he was a good friend to the private soldier and much sentiment clung round the famous white coat and the whiter whiskers and moustache, which were always, like the *Oriflamme*, in the thickest of the battle.

In the following month Havelock had other worries to distract his mind. His daughter was ill and the doctors told him that she must go back to England. Somehow he raised enough money to pay the passage and Hannah and the children sailed at the end of the month. He remained at duty all that summer, but he was really ill himself, his liver complaint aggravated by financial strain and by the anxiety about his reprimand. At last he decided that he must listen to the doctors and take the long leave to which he was entitled, however much it would impoverish him. Even now he would have stayed at duty but for the thought of what his family's position would be should he die while in India or be permanently invalided out of the service. In October he sailed for England and arrived in London on 5th November, after an absence of twenty-six years.

They took a small house in Devonshire, near to Plymouth, and he rested there through the winter. They had, he reported, 'ordinances and faithful preaching, no small blessings', but he found the climate enervating and 'the constant rain damp and not very pleasing'. Nor did he like the district, though there were good day schools for the younger children and they found that living was comparatively cheap there. During the winter he paid several visits to London in the interests of his second boy, Joshua, for whom he was trying to get a cadetship in the East India Company. He had expected to meet with a chilly greeting at the Horse Guards, for his reprimand still rankled in his memory, and he was honestly amazed at the warmth of his reception. Lord Hardinge was devoting his retirement to caring for the interests of his old comrades, and the Commander-in-Chief was still the Duke of Wellington, an old and failing man now, but always at the service of another old soldier, who had served his country well. The Duke presented him at a Levée, where he kissed the hand of his Queen, and Hardinge could not do enough for him. He was elected, to his surprise and delight, a member of the United Services Club and invited to the dinner which the club gave to Lord Gough as well as to the banquet with which the East India Company welcomed Gough home. There he was saddened by the sight of the old Duke of Wellington, when he rose to speak.

> 'I never witnessed [he wrote] so affecting a spectacle of mouldering greatness. He is so deaf that he seems to me to utter prolonged inarticulate sounds without being aware of it. He begins, but rarely concludes a sentence, and where he breaks off in a period the spectator doubts from his manner whether he will commence another, or fall down apoplectic in the next effort to begin one.'

England appeared to him to be,

> 'more intensely aristocratic than ever. The great changes are, the rapidity of communication by locomotives, the extraordinary increase in the power of the press, the improved morality and decency of the habits of the middle and lowest classes, and the accumulation of unions for the promotion of industry, comfort and decidedly of religion. . . .'

But he adds that

> 'the wealthy and great, under any pretext, are entirely wrapt up in themselves and their own interests. Avarice is the great idol, greater than fame just now.'

In the following year the Havelocks moved to London for the greater ease of lobbying for Joshua at India House, but the change did not suit Havelock and the doctors sent him to the Continent for a short visit, to drink the waters at Schwallbach Springs, the fashionable spa of the moment, and from there he took the opportunity of visiting the battle-field of Waterloo. Then he was back again in the Bloomsbury house and calling on the Directors of the East India Company. Lord Hardinge, who had influence everywhere, used it unsparingly at India House and Joshua got his cadetship. His father regarded it as a great triumph, since he was a Queen's and not a Company's officer and had therefore less claim on their generosity, but his gratitude did not prevent him from shrewdly observing the organisation and methods of the Company and of expressing some criticism of them in private letters. He felt, he admitted, that

> 'the intervention of the Court [of Directors] as a body between the Ministers and India is advantageous to the country as preventing party influence reaching it, saving the patronage being entirely jobbed away for votes in Parliament, and affording a chance of some knowledge of India being brought to the task of governing it. . . . But [he adds severely], the privileges of the proprietors of stock are a pure and unmixed mischief. As a Court, their proceedings are and always have been absolutely ridiculous;

as a constituency, they are disposed to elect jobbers than the many great and good men who have subserved the interests of their country in India, and would display the most useful talent in managing its affairs, if they belonged to its home government. The Company has long ceased to trade, yet the city interest continues to return merchants, bankers, shipowners and captains, with now and then a petulant old soldier, who never commanded in any battle in India, but is connected with the proprietorial families.'

But the Company dealt fairly with him and he had the satisfaction of knowing that when his time came to return to India, two of his sons would be serving their country there—Henry with the 10th Foot and Joshua in the Company's service in Bombay.

The family went for a holiday in Belgium and Germany and he visited the battlefield of Leipsic, but their enjoyment was marred by one more disappointment over the matter of promotion.

One of the lieutenant-colonels of his regiment was ready to sell out and he had the purchase money ready, but found that he was too late. A junior major in the Regiment had already paid over the purchase money before the resignation was announced. Havelock could have asserted his seniority and insisted on his own offer being accepted, but he did not feel that he could do it. Major Mansfield had offered—and paid—more than the regulation price, and Havelock could not bring himself to insist on the acceptance of a lower offer; he certainly could not raise his own bid, since he had only been able to find the money by the kindness of an old friend.

'It would [he said] have been hard on old Byrne, who is about half a degree more broken than myself, to stop the purchase at this stage and, if I taken the Lieutenant-Colonelcy, it must have been at the expense of Major Mansfield, who had without reservation paid for it heavily in hard cash, and would not have got it after all. . . . I suppose [he adds bitterly] thereafter I shall see some youth of some sixteen years' standing in the army gazetted over my head.'

He refers in the same letter to an earlier remark of his, that he had been 'purchased over by three sots and two fools' and tries to comfort himself with the reflection that 'it is a pleasant variety to be superseded by a man of sense and gentlemanly habits'.

It was cold comfort for a major of over fifty years of age, and for a short time he had thoughts of retiring, since he felt that he would never get any further up the ladder. 'If', he wrote, 'I had no family to support and the right of choice in my hands, I would not serve an hour longer.' But the right was not in his hands, nor, he felt, was the decision his own. 'The thing is of the Lord.'

Hope rose again when he was at Bonn in August, with the rumour that there was to be a Brevet List in November, in which four or five Queen's A.D.C.s were to be appointed major-generals and so have to vacate their positions. He was not without hope that one of the vacancies so created might fall to his share, and wrote to friends in England to invite their good offices. Characteristically he shrank from putting himself forward for a position so closely connected with his Queen, but he was so desperate that he could see no other way by which he could hope to get promotion, and he knew that, for an officer who was on service in India, attendance at Court was dispensed with. His letters on the subject make clear his repugnance at what seems to him a proof of ambition, and also that it was only for the sake of his family that he had hardened his heart.

Again he was to be disappointed, for the rumour proved to be an empty one, and he resigned himself to return to India and take his chance of promotion while on service there. He returned to England to take farewell of his family and friends. Hannah had been anxious to accompany him, but, with what sad reluctance it may be imagined, he had dissuaded her. The children were happy at school in England, and were getting an infinitely better education than would be possible in India. He returned to Bonn and travelled thence across Europe, stopping to look at several more battlefields, and visiting the picture galleries at Dresden and Vienna. He was better in health than he had been for years but he trailed a sad and heavy heart across Europe and every letter to his wife speaks of the bitterness of their separation—'the bitterness of parting, my position after so many years, which renders it unavoidable'. He was going back to duty as unwillingly as ever did little boy go back to school. India held nothing for him now but a continuance of routine duties as a regimental officer with little hope of promotion and no certainty of a staff appointment—nothing but ten or fifteen years of service, of being passed over by his juniors, of living like a pauper and saving every penny that he could spare, with a further prospect of spending his last years in a cheap neighbourhood in England, trying to launch his family into the world on a major's pension. All that he cared for now was left behind in England. He must have known that the chances of military life might go against him and that he might never see his wife and children again. There would be no need of second-sight, no presentiment to tell him that. He had seen Broadfoot and Sale die in action, and many others struck down by the cholera or dysentery. There is no need to attribute to him any further sight into the future than any other officer of his experience might have when he ended his last letter written to his wife before reaching India:

> 'Now—though the word tears my heart-strings—adieu! May God grant us a happy meeting sooner than we expect! but if never on Earth, in the presence of Jesus, I trust we shall meet.'

CHAPTER XI

THE GREASED CARTRIDGES (1852–1853)

HAVELOCK RETURNED in December 1852 to an India at peace with her neighbours and within her own borders: an India, too, which, under Lord Dalhousie's enlightened rule, was slowly moving in the direction of prosperity and tranquillity in home affairs. Dalhousie was a wise and enthusiastic reformer and he was pressing on with his improvements in transport and communications and with his unswerving intention to extend to India all the blessings of a civilised rule. At the same time the power and possessions of the British Raj continued to grow in majesty and wealth as first the Punjab, then Sind and Oudh were annexed by the Crown and became British possessions. Men like Henry Lawrence and Outram looked on these proceedings with some misgivings, and Dalhousie himself was not convinced of the necessity or the advisability of annexing Oudh, but the Company insisted and he felt it to be his duty to obey. He was not always happy in his choice of methods and some of his acts, such as the Enam Commission, which was set up to enquire into the titles of land-owners in Oudh, gave great offence, especially among those whose titles to the land which they possessed would least bear investigation. One act of his, which seemed to be quite unimportant at the time yet was to have far-reaching and evil effects, was the refusal of a pension to the son of the Peishwa of Bithur. The old Peishwa, having been removed from his position, had been granted a handsome pension by the British and, when he died and his adopted son succeeded him, formal application was made for the continuance of the pension. Dalhousie refused it rather peremptorily, though with good reason, and so made a lasting enemy, who, under the better-known name of the Nana Sahib, was to do terrible harm to the British at Cawnpore.

Only a few months after Havelock's return to duty in India, the first issue of the new Enfield rifle began to the native troops and the new cartridges with them, in small quantities for instruction and practice. Until then the native regiments had been armed with the smooth-bored musket, long famous as Brown Bess, but the British Government had been carrying out tests with the Minié and Enfield rifles and had decided on the Enfield. Its peculiarity was that it needed a greased cartridge, the end of which had to be bitten or torn off by the rifleman when loading, and tests had proved that biting was the quicker and more efficient method. The earliest cartridges were greased with lard or mutton fat or, less often, with beef fat. It mattered of course nothing to the European which was used. But the authorities at home had overlooked the fact that the taste and touch of hogsflesh were defilement to the Mohammedan and that the cow was a sacred animal to the Hindu.

When the first cartridges were issued for test in India in 1853, Colonel Tucker, who was then Adjutant-General of the Bengal Army, was alert enough instantly to suspect the trouble which the grease might cause and reported his fears to the military board at Calcutta, recommending that none of the cartridges should be issued until the Board had satisfied themselves that the greasing was such as to give no offence and were in a position to assure the troops of it. Unhappily the report was treated as a piece of fanciful nonsense from an over-suspicious officer and no action was taken. Indeed the Board thought so little of it that they did not find it worth while to mention it to the Governor-General. As it happened, when the cartridges were issued, it never occurred to the Sepoys to question the composition of the grease and there was no hesitation about using them. Even three years later—and only a year before the outbreak of the Mutiny—when manufacture of the cartridges began in India, Brahmin factory workers at Meerut handled the grease without question. It was not until in 1857, when a chance remark from a Lascar, at the factory at Dum-Dum, made the workers aware that they had been handling unclean flesh, that any feeling arose against the cartridges. By that time the Sepoy Army was ready to listen to any rumour and act upon it.

To all appearance the Sepoy Army which Havelock saw on his return was as well disciplined and as loyal as it had been when he had left for England two years before. Certainly there was no feeling among the regimental officers, who naturally knew the men best, that any trouble was brewing. There had, it was true, been one or two incidents during the last few years which suggested that there was a bad feeling in some regiments, but there had always been incidents since the days of Clive, and nothing had come of them. These last had yielded to reason or force, and the general heart of the Sepoys was as good as ever.

But Havelock had been a staff-officer and his various appointments had brought him into contact with men of high rank and long experience, who looked at the Sepoy with eyes unclouded by regimental sentiment and loyalty. In talk with them he learned that the incidents had not been as few or as trivial as he had been given to suppose. There had been a dangerous situation just after the second Sikh war, when two regiments at Rawalpindi had made a disturbance over the withdrawal of the cash allowances for foreign service. Sir Colin Campbell had been in command there, while Sir Charles Napier was C.-in-C. India, and, on Napier's orders, Campbell had dealt with the trouble by a combination of patient reasoning and overwhelming display of force. Napier had taken the matter very seriously and when, shortly afterwards, he went on a tour of the Northern Provinces, he instituted close enquiries into the state of feeling in all the Native regiments there. The result was alarming, for he had reason to believe that twenty-four regiments were disaffected and were only waiting for an opportunity to mutiny. Before long he had proof that his information was accurate. In December 1849 a mutiny at Wazirabad was only averted by the tact and wit of Colonel Hearsey, who knew and understood the Sepoy as well as any officer in India.

Napier was by this time convinced that a serious outbreak was imminent in the Northern Provinces and made arrangements to meet it. He established a temporary headquarters at Peshawar and concentrated several European regiments there. But, when the outbreak came, it came so suddenly that he could not deal with it personally and it was suppressed not by a British regiment but by the 1st Native Cavalry. The 66th Native Infantry mutinied at Govindur and confidently called on their comrades of the 1st Cavalry to join them, but the cavalry not only refused but rode down the mutinous regiment and inflicted casualties. Napier hurried to the town, rewarded the loyal cavalry and disbanded the 66th, boasting a little unwisely that he had taught the Brahmins that, if ever they gave trouble, a more warlike people were always ready and able to deal with them. The trouble seemed to be over, but unfortunately Napier's next action brought him into collision with the Governor-General. Napier had never concealed his opinion that the Government's policy of whittling down the Sepoys' allowances was mean and unworthy and a certain source of unrest. On his own responsibility, he restored some of their losses in the form of an old allowance which had been granted to the Sepoys in the past, in compensation for dearness of provisions. The Governor-General was at the moment absent from the seat of Government at Calcutta and Napier gave orders that the allowance was to be paid until he had returned and could give his own decision on the case. Dalhousie, on his return, read Napier's report and was furious. He did not believe that the outbreak at Govindur had been serious and held that Napier had exceeded his powers in a way that amounted to a direct challenge to himself.

Able and farseeing though Dalhousie was, he was arrogant and overquick to suspect and resent a personal slight and he chose the worst possible way of putting the C.-in-C. in his place. He countermanded the order for payment and publicly rebuked Napier, in terms which would have been offensive if addressed to an impertinent subaltern. Napier, who was as hot-headed and obstinate as Dalhousie, bitterly resented the insult and there was some acrimonious correspondence between them, at the end of which Napier contemptuously threw up his command. Both of them were so set upon their rights that they gave no thought to the folly and lack of dignity which their public argument displayed, and the unfriendly part of the Native army looked on with delight. They came to two conclusions—firstly, that the Government were determined to cheat them of all their just dues, one after another, and secondly, that even the C.-in-C. India had no real power and was liable to be disowned and chastised by his civilian masters—and if the C.-in-C. could be so treated, it followed that their own regimental officers counted for nothing.

The next incident came in 1852 and involved the 38th Bengal Native Infantry, who had been invited to volunteer for service in Burma. Most of the men were Brahmins to whom it was forbidden to cross the 'Black Water' and they refused to believe that the invitation to volunteer was genuine, suspecting that, if they did not volunteer, they would be shipped overseas by compulsion. They refused duty and there was nothing else to do but to disband them.

The incident had happened while Havelock was on his way out to India and, on his arrival, he found it the chief topic of discussion in every Mess which he visited. The general feeling of the senior officers with whom he discussed it was that, while there was no reason to suspect the Madras and Bombay troops, the Bengal Army was in an explosive state and that some radical reform was needed. In Madras and Bombay the caste feeling was not nearly so strong as in Bengal and there were few Brahmins among the men. It had been the steady policy of every Governor since the days of Clive to pay all possible respect to caste and not to upset any tradition or feeling about it in the high-caste regiments. The army had accepted the custom but, as time went on, they began to see that, while it was laudable as a principle, it was unworkable from a practical standpoint. An army which could not be compelled to serve wherever its services were required, in which, whatever the urgency of a crisis might be, the regiments had to be begged to volunteer for service overseas, was an army only in name, and discipline in a unit where a low-caste sergeant was obliged to cringe before a high-caste private was a mockery of the name of discipline. Year after year, Commanders-in-Chief had urged the iniquity of the system on their civilian superiors, pleading for a reform of the Bengal force, by which it could be ruled solely by military discipline and not by caste. There was nothing unfair about their request. The men enlisted voluntarily and every man should know that by enlisting he bound himself to obey his military superiors without question and to serve wherever he was sent. The men who were already serving could and should be offered the choice between staying in the army under the new discipline or taking their discharge. But the officers pleaded in vain. The respect for caste had become a Governmental policy, hallowed by tradition and preserved from the sacrilege of discussion or the intrusion of common sense. All the officers got was the typical answer of weak and obstinate Authority—'It is a matter of Policy and we cannot discuss it.'

Dalhousie was as intransigent on this point as any of his predecessors, but he realised that one thing which was necessary was an alteration in the comparative strength of the British and Native troops in India. Towards the end of his administration the Native troops outnumbered the British by a proportion of nearly five to one. 'India', it was commonly said, 'is held by a Corporal's Guard.' And the difference was made more glaring and more dangerous by the haphazard system of distributing the British regiments among the districts. In 1857 there was only one British regiment in all the 500 miles between Calcutta and Allahabad, and Delhi, where there was a huge arsenal, had no British garrison at all, whereas in some stations, such as Meerut, several British units were concentrated in a small area.

With a modern army it would have been a thoroughly sensible arrangement, since the concentrated troops could have been kept mobile and held ready to reinforce any point where trouble might arise. But the army in India in the middle of the nineteenth century relied on no motive power other than the feet of the infantry and the horses of the artillery and cavalry, except on rare occasions when a unit might be carried in bullock carts commandeered from the countryside, or occasionally when it was possible to embark a battalion in boats and send them by river to some fortunately situated spot, as, in fact, some of Havelock's reinforcements were sent in 1857.

Dalhousie was alive to the evil of the shortage of British troops and of their faulty distribution and it is to his credit that he took what steps he could to remedy it. He wrote a detailed and admirably argued report to the Court of Directors, urging the immediate need for an alteration in the strength of both Queen's and Company's troops. It does not appear from the report that he was thinking of any danger from mutiny of the Native force. His argument is based on the enormous increase of garrison duties which the recent annexations entailed on the army and on the danger of attack from outside India by enemies, who might easily think that the army was too widespread and too fully committed to offer any real resistance. He envisaged attacks from the rulers of Afghanistan, Nepal or Burma. What he did not envisage was trouble on a big scale from the Native Army itself. He can hardly be blamed for that, since it was a military rather than a civilian problem, but he would have been wise to listen more attentively to the warnings of experienced soldiers such as Napier. Unfortunately Napier, who saw the danger, was not the most tactful of men and he personally disliked Dalhousie, so that they could never really get together for consultation.

Whatever arguments Dalhousie might have used would have been equally unavailing in the board-room of the Company, where the only prevailing thought was of cost and profit. Any reform would cost a vast amount of money, and dangers which loomed large in Meerut and Benares were hardly visible in Leadenhall Street. The Court emphatically refused to consider any scheme of reform. They would not pay for it in cash and left their servants in India to pay for it in lives and property a few years later. It is only justice that the result of this policy in the Mutiny led to the Company's loss of control when in 1858 India passed under the direct rule of Her Majesty.

CHAPTER XII

QUARTERMASTER-GENERAL (1853–1857)

THERE HAD been so many set-backs and disappointments in Henry Havelock's career, that it is pleasant to learn that during the last few years of his life his luck changed altogether for the better. On his return to India there was no sign of the change, but it had in fact begun late in the year before when Lord Hardinge became Commander-in-Chief of the British Army after the Duke of Wellington's death. Havelock was a Queen's officer and appointments in the Queen's Army were controlled by the Horse Guards and not by the authorities in India. He had served under Hardinge and there was a mutual trust and admiration between them. Havelock could be sure that he would not be overlooked for any suitable appointment. At the beginning of 1853, only a month after he had landed, the second Burmese war broke out, and as nothing else offered, he applied for a staff appointment, being quite ready, as he said, old as he was, 'at the shortest notice for an encounter with the new generation of Woongees, Muha Mengees, Muha Thilwas, Bundoolas or Tharawaddys'. His application did not reach Lord Dalhousie, who was acting as his own war minister, until all the appointments had been settled.

The war lasted only eight months and by that time Havelock had brighter prospects in view. He had been immensely cheered by the news of his son Henry's selection as Adjutant of his regiment, the 10th Foot. The boy, his father considered, 'ought to be very glad to get that at twenty-two which I accepted thankfully at forty'. Once again there was talk in the army of a winter Brevet List and Havelock, knowing the strength of his claim to be included, wrote to Lord Hardinge at the Horse Guards. To modern ideas, there seems something almost shameless in the way that he pushed his claims to advancement on every possible opportunity, but the army of that time saw nothing odd in it. It was almost the only way in which a non-purchase officer could hope to overcome the slow wait for a vacancy, and such an officer saw nothing shameful in talking about his 'military patron'. Nor was it only the non-purchase officers who looked after their own interests, though the more favoured and monied men might use a slightly less crude form of approach. But such delicate methods as a word with a man at the club, a hint from a noble relative, an entertainment for a general's womenfolk were not for officers whose only qualification was their fitness for the job. Lord Hardinge took it as the most natural thing in the world that Havelock should write to him, and even that Marshman, who was returning to England on leave, should ask for an interview to press his brother-in-law's claim. Once more there was no Brevet List, but the letter to Hardinge bespoke his interest in a more important matter, since there would very soon be a vacancy in the really important position of Adjutant-General to the Queen's Troops in India. There were two other candidates in the field, either of whom looked a more likely winner, and Hardinge's reply was friendly but non-committal. At the interview with Marshman, he admitted frankly that in his opinion Havelock's claims were very strong, and that he had himself recommended him for the post in 1849, after Colonel Cureton's death at Ramnuggur, but the other candidates, Colonel Markham and Colonel Lugard, were both excellent officers and were both being supported by influential people. Markham was an A.D.C. to the Queen, which seemed to give him prior right and Lugard was backed by the C.-in-C. India, and was temporarily holding the appointment. The general opinion was that Markham would be the lucky man and Havelock shared it. Writing to Marshman to thank him for his efforts, he said:

> 'Nevertheless, I see beyond a doubt that Markham is to be the man. He is the son of a bishop, I believe, or an archbishop, who was a tutor to some of the Royal Family, and is, moreover, backed by Lord Raglan. I saw him at Bombay and a fine chivalrous fellow he certainly is: and we fully agreed that we were not to quarrel about it, whoever might be appointed.'

Rumour and Havelock were right and, somewhat against his will, Lord Hardinge found himself obliged to appoint Markham. Like the good-hearted friend that he was, he instantly took steps to provide for the disappointed candidates. Lugard was made an A.D.C. to the Queen and sent to Bombay as Deputy Adjutant-General; and Havelock was given the appointment of Quartermaster-General of the Queen's Troops in India. With his usual humility, Havelock wrote:

'I am appointed the successor of Nicholls, Whittingham and Sale, an elevation which I did not look for, when I was lackeying at the heels of the last-named, as his adjutant, or writing his despatches. I thank God for the provision which this, in His goodness, promises for my family. . . . I must hasten to say that, if the Bengal pay and audit book and my recollections are to be trusted, the pay is precisely the same as that of Adjutant-General. I may reckon it an additional mercy that, in my sixtieth year I am, for once in my life, to have no work, with nearly £3,000 a year.'

He must indeed have felt that he had sailed into calm waters, for his duties, as he wrote, were

'literally nil. . . . My work averages two returns and two letters per mensem: but time never hangs heavily on my hands. I ride when it does not rain a deluge, and, when it does, I am never without indoor occupation. Books attract me even more than when I was a boy.'

In this pleasant life and in the atmosphere of success, his nature expanded into a geniality which he had aways had to repress in the stern struggle for existence. He was still saving money for his family and for his retirement, but he was at last in the happy situation of not having to count every penny and could allow himself some comforts and even small luxuries. Like most men, he was the better for them. All his life he had kept away from society, not because he disliked his fellow men, but simply because he would not accept hospitality which he could not afford to return. But now he was living at the Military Club and could take part in the more modest of its entertainments. His old friend Lieutenant-Colonel Balcarres Ramsay of the 75th Foot has left a genial picture of him in his *Rough Recollections of Military Service and Society*:

'It has been the custom to consider General Havelock as simply a stern Puritan General. Stern as a disciplinarian he undoubtedly was, Puritan as regards the purity of his motives and actions he undoubtedly was. He lived the life, therefore his influence was great. . . . I saw a great deal of him then and liked him more and more every day. He had a great deal of kindly humour about him and was much liked by many wild youngsters who were not in the least of his way of thinking. He mixed freely with the members, dining at our table-d'hôte and enjoying his cool glass of wine as much as anyone else. . . . I mention these little traits of character, as I know it has been represented that Havelock was a morose, gloomy puritan and water-drinker. Nothing could be further from the fact. Certainly he was a devoted Christian: and if you went into his room or tent at any time, you would see his Bible, which he constantly studied, lying open: but this made him neither morose nor ascetic. On the contrary he mixed freely in society and enjoyed it very much.'

The truth was that Havelock—as all men with a settled faith must be—was fundamentally a happy man. So far he had only allowed himself to relax and be at ease among his own family, but his success released his capacity for enjoyment and the goodness of his heart, of which his devotion to his wife and children was such abundant proof, helped him to make friends. He had always loved his fellows, as a Christian should, and done his best for them. Hundreds of men in the 13th Foot bore witness to that. Now he found that he liked them as friends and that they responded by liking him. It was late in life for him to make the discovery, but some men never make it at all.

There was further good fortune in store for him. Colonel Markham had only held the position of Adjutant-General for a few months when he was promoted to Major-General and had to vacate the appointment, to take up one fitting for his rank. Lord Hardinge, who never forgot a promise or a friend, instantly appointed Havelock to succeed him. There was a touch of irony in the fact that Havelock's seniority was now such that he was nearly due for promotion himself, and in that case could not have accepted the post. A little skilful manipulation of dates by the Horse Guards put back his seniority by a year or two and he went happily off to Calcutta to report to the new C.in-C. India, General Anson. Before he left Bombay, he wrote to his wife in an unusual tone of gaiety,

> 'Here we are, on our way to the City of Palaces. I only wait to see my ponderous office establishment fairly started by bullock train, to be off myself in the somewhat lighter carriage, which may carry me in six days to General Anson's ante-chamber.'

He arrived in Calcutta on 24th January, 1856, and at last he could feel tolerably certain of his future. By Lord Hardinge's kindness, he was assured of a full five years' tenure of the Adjutant-Generalship, and, as his Brevet Colonelcy had now come through and was followed almost at once by his substantive promotion to that rank, he could count on becoming a major-general when it was time for him to vacate his appointment. He was still sailing in calm waters.

But, though neither he nor anyone else realised it at the time, the calm was only on the surface. 1856 was the last year of Lord Dalhousie's Governor-Generalship and the year of the annexation of the Kingdom of Oudh, and Oudh was the home of some 40,000 of the

Sepoys in the Bengal Army. In Bithur, the Nana Sahib was nursing his hatred of the English, who had refused him a pension, and throughout the province dispossessed and threatened land-holders were plotting for the recovery of their privileges. In that year the General Service Order was published, which made the whole Native army liable for service wherever they might be sent, and not only were all new recruits to be enlisted on that basis, but men already serving were affected by the same order though they had enlisted voluntarily, perhaps many years before, on the understanding that they would not be made to cross the 'Black Water' against their will and the prohibition of their caste.

Lord Dalhousie resigned on 26th February of this year and Lord Canning had been chosen to succeed him. A few months before his departure from England, Canning had been entertained at a banquet by the East India Company and during his speech had spoken some words which were long to be remembered in India.

> 'We must not forget that, in the sky of India, serene as it is, a small cloud may arise, at first no bigger than a man's hand, but which, growing larger and larger, may at last threaten to burst and overwhelm us with ruin.'

Dalhousie's period of rule had indeed been the high noon of the British Raj. 1856 was to be the short tropical twilight before the fall of darkness and already the shadows were lengthening. The rest of Canning's speech seems to show that he was thinking of dangers from without rather than from within, and these dangers were sapping—had already sapped—some of the strength which would be needed for the danger at home. Britain had just emerged from a bloody and useless war in the Crimea with diminished strength and lowered prestige. Not even the infantry's gallantry at the Alma and Inkermann, the dogged endurance in the freezing winter before Sebastopol, not even the glory of the Heavy and Light Brigades at Balaclava could hide the futility of British strategy and tactics and the incompetence of British administration. The story lost nothing in the telling as it ran through the cantonments in India, where gloating Sepoys once more hailed the end of the Feringhees' power. The Crimea had brought into the light of day the imperative need for drastic reforms in the army, but time was too short to allow of their having any effect within the few months of peace which were left to India. The army there would have to face their ordeal with a supply and transport system such as their fellows had endured in 1854.

In this year of 1856 too, for their further embarrassment, the diplomats and statesmen had blundered into a trivial and unnecessary squabble in China, which drew off a sorely needed force, for Herat. Lord Canning succeeded to an inheritance more ominous than had faced any Governor-General since the days of Warren Hastings. He was about as far as possible from being the man whom the British would, had they known what was in store, have chosen to carry the heavy burden.

Yet, though that is the truth and soon everyone realised it, such a consensus of opinion involves Canning in no discredit. He was a man who in normal times had every quality needed to make him one of the outstanding Governors. He was upright, brave, unsparing of effort, just and merciful. He came from Eton and Christ Church, where he had been a good classical scholar, with a bent towards philosophy, and he had a great gift for friendship. His tragedy was that he had an excess of all these good qualities at a time when the only qualities which were vital were just those which his nature withheld from him. He was so scrupulous, so intent on justice, that he would never decide on any case until he had carefully studied all sides of it and heard all available points of view. He was not unable to make up his mind or to hold to it when made up, but he could not bring himself to give a rapid decision which might involve, however, remotely, injustice to any man. Before he had been in office for a year, he came to be known as 'Clemency Canning'. It was a name which did him honour, though there was derision in the giving of it, since he showed clemency at a moment when the meaning of the word had all but passed from men's memories.

Half-way through the year the Commander-in-Chief India and his staff were occupied by the probability of war in Persia, and with the preparation of an expeditionary force. There had been constant friction over the possession of Herat almost continuously during the last few years, and in British minds, the fear of Russia was always behind it. The Persians had occupied it, abandoned it and occupied it again and their latest threat had been in the last month of 1855. There had been months of dilatory and unsuccessful negotiations in Constantinople, which broke down finally in the early summer of the following year, when the Persians began to prepare another invasion. In July the British Foreign Office despaired of settling the difficulty by peaceful means and ordered the Governor-General of India to prepare a force sufficient to occupy the island of Kharak and the city and district of Bushire, in the Persian Gulf, and to be ready to march in September. There was a last useless attempt at negotiation and in November war was declared.

The first division of the British force in Persia, about four thousand men under General Stalker, opened hostilities on 29th November, by occupying Bushire, after it had been bombarded by a naval squadron. Anson, the C.-in-C. India, was collecting a second division to bring the expeditionary force up to its full strength. He consulted Havelock, his Adjutant-General, about the appointment of a general officer to take command of both divisions, and Havelock at once recommended Sir James Outram, then serving at Bombay. Anson approved and further gave his consent when Outram asked Havelock to go with him as commander of the Bombay Division. The invitation implied a great compliment as Havelock was a Bengal officer and it was rarely that an officer from one Presidency was offered the command of troops from another. He telegraphed an immediate acceptance and wrote to his wife:

> 'The command is responsible but my trust is in God, . . . I should never have solicited such a command, and would, in truth, rather have been employed in the north-west provinces, where it is not unlikely that a force may hereafter be employed. But when the post of honour and danger was offered to me by telegraph, old as I am, I did not hesitate a moment. The wires carried back my unconditional and immediate acceptance.'

He wasted no time on his journey. He left Agra on 12th January, 1857, and, according to his schedule, he should have arrived in Bombay on the 26th. But Havelock's ideas of rapid movement were different from the accepted ideas of most senior officers. He travelled by day and night, mostly in a mail-cart without any springs, averaging 100 miles a day, and was in Bombay five days before they expected him there. Outram had sailed on the 19th, but, though Havelock was ready to follow on the 22nd, he was delayed for a week by a breakdown in the engines of the steamer, and he sailed at last on the 29th. By that time his promotion had come through and, as he sailed out of the harbour at Bombay, he heard, for the first time, the harbour guns booming out the salute for a brigadier-general.

CHAPTER XIII

THE PERSIAN WAR (1857)

AS THE ships sailed northwards towards the Persian Gulf, through the short winter days and long dark nights, there were strange rumours abroad in the country which they had left, strange passing of messages, secret and furtive meetings and colloquies in village and cantonment. Night after night, native runners came into the villages of Oudh and Bengal, bearing the flat dough-cakes which the Indians called chupatties. They gave these to the headman of the village, bidding him prepare four more and send them out to near-by villages. The origin of the chupatty as a symbol of uprising has never to this day been satisfactorily explained, nor the message which it carried truly interpreted, but all authorities agree that it was some acknowledged form of summons calling to the Hindus to be ready for an uprising, much as was the Fiery Cross to the Highlanders in the days of Montrose and Dundee.

If the chupatty was the sign to the people of the villages and the towns, the mysterious message of the Lotos flower was as obviously meant for the Sepoy. At military stations all over the north-west and north-east of India there were reports of the passing of a flower through the ranks of the Native regiments. Officers reported that the lotos flowers were brought to their lines by runners from other regiments, often from a great distance. The flowers were handed to the senior Native officer, who touched them and sent them along the lines until every Sepoy had seen and touched them. Certain officers, curious but not alarmed, asked the meaning of this strange ritual, and were put off with denials or with vague tales of greetings from one regiment to another, and since, on the whole, the British officers still believed implicitly in the loyalty of their 'baba-log', they were easily appeased and thought no more of it. Historians, examining and comparing the tales many years afterwards, have been equally mystified, but on the whole inclined to believe that the chupatty and the lotos flower were the signs for the beginning of a concerted rising of army and people, which never really came to life. Had it been thoroughly organised and well timed, it must surely have been the end of the British Raj. British resources were strained almost beyond breaking point by a mutiny which was confined to the troops in the Bengal Presidency and in which the people of India took scarcely any part. As it was, the odds against the British were about five to one. Had the troops from Madras and Bombay presidencies joined in, the odds would have been doubled, and if there had been a concerted rising of the people at the same time, the Corporal's Guard would have been overwhelmed in a few weeks. Their salvation lay in the fact that there were no guiding hand and brain behind the movement, that outbreaks were spasmodic and not synchronised, and that there were enough differences of feeling, religion and caste among the natives to prevent a real combination. The Mohammedan ideal was a revival of the old Empire of the Moguls, with Delhi for their capital. The greater part of the Hindu troops came from Oudh and were drawn back to it in the hope of avenging the recent annexation and recovering the sequestrated lands. Neither section of the army had enough sympathy with the other to forgo their own objectives for the sake of combination.

Havelock had left Bombay on 29th January, 1857. Owing to defective engines and heavy weather the ship made slow progress and did not reach Bushire, in the Persian Gulf, until 15th February. By that time, the first outbreaks had begun among the Sepoy Army in Bengal.

On 22nd January, 1857, Captain Wright, an instructor at the musketry depôt at Dum-Dum, reported to Major Bontein, the Commandant, a curious incident which had been brought to his notice. Dum-Dum contained, besides the musketry depôt, the great arsenal, with its laboratory and workshops, where the ammunition for the Bengal troops was made, and at which the new greased cartridges for the Enfield rifles were being prepared. There were high-caste Brahmins among the workers, and on that January day, as one of them was coming away from his work, he was accosted by a sweeper—the lowest caste of all India—who asked for a drink of water from his lotah, the brass drinking vessel which the Hindus carried. The Brahmin refused indignantly, since the touch of a sweeper's lips would be unspeakable defilement to his caste, but the sweeper flung back at him the taunt that he and his like would soon have no caste at all, since they had been handling the fat of cows. There had been rumours of the use of animal fat before, but now the thing had been spoken openly and the story ran through the native lines at every cantonment. By the end of the month four native regiments at Barrackpore, near Calcutta, were out of hand and insubordinate and within a day or two they were setting fire to officers' bungalows and European property. The infection spread to Burhampore, where, a few days later, the first act of mutiny was reported. The 19th Native Regiment of Foot refused to accept the cartridges for musketry practice. There could be no ignoring or passing over of such an open act of mutiny, but at the moment the Government of India was helpless, since they had not a single regiment of British troops available to suppress the mutiny, without sending for one from such a distance that prompt action was out of the question.

Canning acted as promptly as could anyone in the circumstances, by sending for the 84th Queen's Regiment, who were in Burma, 800 miles away from the seat of trouble. General Hearsey, a brave and devoted officer, who had spent his life in the army in India and knew the Sepoys better than any man then serving, went out to Barrackpore and did his best to reason with and persuade the mutineers, who gave him a hearing and offered no harm, but remained obstinate in refusing duty. As the days passed and the 84th were toiling wearily from their far-off station, the Sepoys took heart and began to believe that nothing would happen and that the arm of the Feringhees had lost its length and their hand its power. Twelve days later—just a week after Havelock had landed at Bushire—a private in the 34th Native Regiment, while on guard duty at Barrackpore, fired at the adjutant of the regiment, wounding him and killing his horse. There are a few occasions in history when the name of a quite undistinguished person suddenly attains to general fame—a fame which lasts long after its owner has sunk back into his natural obscurity. It was so with the Sepoy Mangal Pandi, because of whom the British troops ever afterwards gave to the mutineers the name of Pandies. There was a native guard at the barrack gate under a native officer, but not a man of them moved to help the fallen adjutant and, in a moment, the guard began to batter him with the butts of their muskets. Fortunately General Hearsey rode up almost at once and, being a man of prompt decision, forced the guard at the point of his revolver to help the adjutant and to arrest Pandi, who tried unsuccessfully to shoot himself. Hearsey knew the necessity of quick justice when dealing with native troops and within a week Pandi had been court-martialled and hanged. Unhappily, Hearsey's summary powers did not run to the punishment of native officers and the case of the guard commander and his men was referred to General H.Q. It was then that the Army began to realise the fatal effects of the Governor-General's judicial mind and fear of injustice, and also of the merciful temper which won for him the name of 'Clemency Canning'. The native officer was not tried until 11th April nor executed till the 21st. Worse still, when sentence was promulgated on the mutineers of the 19th, the British were staggered to learn that the only punishment which Canning had ordered was the disbanding of the regiment.

The tale of this leniency was soon the common talk of the native lines in every cantonment in the presidency, and a European officer in Oudh reported that one of his native subordinates had asked him whether it was true that the mutinous regiment had not only merely been disbanded but had been paid up to the day of their disbanding.

The news reached Outram and Havelock while they were still in Persia, though the war was over and terms of peace had been agreed at Paris on 4th April. Both of them, with their wealth of experience in dealing with Sepoys, were deeply shocked by this failure to stamp heavily on the first signs of trouble. Havelock wrote later, when drawing up a memorandum on the beginning of the Mutiny:

> 'There must be no more disbandments for mutiny. Mutineers must be attacked and annihilated; and if they are few in any regiment, and not immediately denounced to be shot or hanged, the whole regiment must be deemed guilty and given up to prompt military execution. . . . But much depends on prompt action. The time for threats and promises is gone by; the slightest overt act must be followed by the same retribution which in 1824 Sir Edward Paget dealt out to the 47th Native Infantry, thereby putting back the Bengal Mutiny eighteen years.'

Neither Havelock nor Outram was merciless by nature, but both of them knew that an apparent act of mercy at a critical moment was certain to bring after it heavy consequences and the need for greater severities.

When the news reached them, they were in the delta of the Euphrates. The first weeks of the war had been spent in the district of Bushire and Kush-Ab, on the eastern shore of the Persian Gulf. The Persians had abandoned the defended position at Braxjun without firing a shot, and though, when on 8th February they were brought to action at Kush-Ab, they had an army of 8,000 foot and 3,000 horse, they made so little attempt to fight that the British drove them headlong in rout while only suffering casualties themselves in killed and wounded of 83 of all ranks.

The Persians were in full retreat and Outram, in the hope of catching them from another direction, re-embarked his force and transported them across the gulf to the mouth of the Euphrates, and prepared for an assault on Mohumbra, another defended position. The attack was to be delivered by Havelock's division who were taken up the river in boats, as the 13th Foot had been conveyed in Burma over thirty years before. The Persians had no stomach for a fight and again abandoned their position without a shot, and, for greater safety, withdrew to the River Karun, a distance of about 100 miles. The war was over and peace was signed on what happened to be Havelock's sixty-second birthday. Appropriately, he got the news just as he was drawing up the troops for church parade on that Sunday morning.

> 'The intelligence [he wrote to his wife] which elevates some and depresses others, finds me calm in my reliance on that dear Redeemer, who has watched over me and cared for me, when I knew Him not, threescore and two years.'

It was difficult to feel much jubilation about the end of a war which had lasted for four months, had cost the British two million pounds, and had achieved nothing except the final destruction of the reputation of the Persian Army. It was followed by news which destroyed even Havelock's calm, when he received a letter, dated 15th March, in which General Anson told him of the mutiny at Burhampore. The authorities at Calcutta were apparently disposed to treat the threat almost with levity, but fortunately Lord Elphinstone, the Governor of Bombay, was more realistic. He sent an urgent message to Outram, asking him to release as many troops as he could spare as quickly as he could, for return to service in India.

Outram acted with equal promptitude, and, though he had arranged to go direct to England on long overdue leave, he cancelled his passage and stayed where he was, to await further orders. The Bombay division, which Havelock had commanded, was hastily thrust into ships and Havelock, finding himself without a command, made his own way to Bombay. He had been so far from the scene of the trouble in India that he naturally did not yet suspect the true import and size of it, and he had it in mind to apply for employment in China. But when he reached Bombay on 29th May, he was greeted by the appalling news of the mutinies at Meerut, Ferozepore and Delhi, and knew that his place was in Bengal, where every available officer and man was desperately needed. The 64th and the 78th Highlanders, who had been part of his division, had been sent straight on by sea to Calcutta, without landing at Bombay.

Reports told of the interruption of communications all over the country and the certainty of delay and probability of destruction if he were to attempt to travel overland back to Calcutta. He embarked on the first available steamer, the *Erin*, on June 1st, hoping to overtake the fast steamer from Suez to Calcutta. On 5th June the *Erin* went aground on the coast of Ceylon, and for a few hours it seemed as if the crew and passengers were doomed. There was a sign of panic among the crew and Havelock took the sensible and characteristic step of securing the store where the spirits were kept and refusing entrance to the frightened men who besieged it. At dawn they managed to get a hawser to land and canoes came out to take off the passengers and crew. As Havelock himself said, 'The madness of man threw us on shore: the mercy of God found us a soft place near Caltura.' As soon as he set foot on shore, he knelt and invited those who were with him to kneel and give thanks to God for their deliverance.

He arrived at Madras on 13th June and learned from the flags of the shipping and of Fort George, which flew at half-mast, that the C.-in-C. India, General Anson, had died of cholera. Anson had been struck down at Ambala while he was on his way to assume command of the troops who were besieging Delhi, and Sir Henry Somerset, the senior officer present there, had taken over the command, while the Government of Bengal had telegraphed to Madras, begging for the services of Sir Patrick Grant, who was in command there, for duty at Calcutta, pending the appointment of a new C.-in-C. Havelock's first intention had been to post across India to join the army before Delhi, but he reflected that he was still Adjutant-General of the Queen's Troops in India, and that his proper place was with the C.-in-C. at Headquarters at Calcutta—the more so because Grant had only just taken over and would be quite unfamiliar with the routine there. Grant was just leaving Madras when Havelock arrived and they travelled together, reaching Calcutta on 17th June. They drove at once to Lord Canning's headquarters and Grant presented Havelock to him with the words, 'Your Excellency, I have brought you the man.'

CHAPTER XIV

MUTINY (1857)

THE OUTBREAKS at Delhi and Meerut in May may be taken as the real starting point of the Sepoy Mutiny. There had been several incidents already but they were isolated and prompt and drastic handling of any of them might have prevented a general outbreak. After May there could be no avoiding it. Delhi had given the mutineers a great arsenal, filled with arms and ammunition of all sorts, but it also gave them something far more important, a cause round which the Mohammedan troops could rally. Delhi was the old seat of the Mogul Empire of Shah Jehan. His last successor still lived there, a senile pensioner who was nothing more than his name, but that name was enough to give a pretence of tradition to a movement. The green flag of Islam flew once more over its fortress and it became the rallying point for the forces who were sworn to drive the Feringhees out of India and re-establish the Empire. It seems unbelievable that the city, with its arsenal, should have been wholly entrusted to the guardianship of Native regiments, except for the small party of Ordnance officers and men who were on duty in the arsenal. However scanty was the British force in the country, it would surely have been only common sense to keep at least one battalion at so important a station, and that lack of foresight was to have disastrous effects. It was to Delhi that many of the mutinous units made their way, after destroying their own cantonments and killing the Europeans there. So it was to Delhi that the 3rd Native Cavalry and the 11th and 20th Infantry came after the murderous affair at Meerut. Meerut too was of particular importance to the successful beginning of the mutiny, because there were several British regiments there at the time.

It was the one place of all where the British might confidently have expected to crush any attempt at revolt, since the European troops comprised cavalry and infantry and all the guns were in European hands. The native troops consisted of one cavalry and two infantry regiments, to whom the British could have opposed the Carabineers, the 60th Rifles and both Field and Horse Artillery; there was ample warning and plenty of time to prepare; the British troops were actually called out to deal with the mutineers; yet in spite of all this the native regiments revolted, committed hideous excesses in the European lines, plundered the treasury and released the prisoners from the gaol, and escaped to Delhi with hardly a single casualty. It was a tragic tale of feeble handling of a crisis, of failure to take responsibility—and ultimately of the British system of allowing senile and incompetent commanders to continue in their posts long after their usefulness, such as it was, had become worn out. They might have taken warning by Elphinstone's failure at Kabul, but the system was too deeply embedded in British military tradition and once more it was to take toll of British lives. Not the least part of the harm which was done at Meerut was the belief, which it instilled into the mutineers there and at Delhi, that the Feringhees were powerless to prevent or to punish any action by native troops. Exaggerated stories of the failure of the British in the Crimea had gone round India, finding ready and credulous hearers in the native lines. After the failure of the British garrison at Meerut, the Sepoys had no further doubt.

On Sunday, as the people came from church at the end of the service, and stood for a few minutes of talk in the churchyard while the gigs were led up to the gate, a bugle sounded harshly in the cavalry lines and there was a rattle of musketry and the drumming of hoofs. The cavalry swept out of their lines and galloped off to the gaol to release the prisoners and the infantry came out to burn and destroy and kill, in the streets and in the European cantonments. The secret had been well kept and the terror was loose. Europeans were hunted down and murdered, the air was full of the crackle of burning timbers and the evening sky darkened with the swirling smoke. The cavalrymen forced the gaol and freed not only their own comrades but every prisoner whom they found there, and from the bazaars, the gutters and the brothels, streamed out every desperate and bloodthirsty ruffian in the town, and many who had been coming into it during the day.

In the European lines the Sepoys burst into the bungalows, cut down women and children, set fire to roof and wall. The British defended themselves as best they could or escaped if they could, all buoyed up by the one hope that any moment they would hear the roar of their guns and see the flashing sabres of the Carabineers. They waited in vain. The British bungalows were some distance away from the soldiers' lines and from the parade ground, yet they could not have failed to hear the guns when they opened fire or the shrill trumpets of the cavalry. But the only sounds were the roar of the flames, the shouts of the murderers and the screams of women and children.

The troops had been called out and Hewitt had arrived to take command, but the situation was too much for him. He did not know what to do, and so did the worst thing which he could have done, which was nothing. In a like position many years before at Vellore, Gillespie had roused a squadron of cavalry and a troop of galloper guns and thundered at full speed right into the heart of the mutineers, trampling, shooting, cutting them down. On the parade ground at Meerut the Rifles and the Carabineers stood in their ranks in the rapidly falling twilight while all round them the fires blazed and the mutineers raged and killed. There was a coming and going of officers and gallopers to and from the spot at one side of the ground where Hewitt sat on his horse, with Archdale Wilson, the Brigadier, and his staff, giving orders and countermanding them, helpless and useless in his senile incompetence. Once he ordered an attack on the native lines, from which all the troops had gone. Wilson was a brave and competent officer and had kept his head, and it was at his often repeated entreaty that Hewitt at last consented to move the troops back towards the European lines for their protection. The moon was up by this time, and by its light the dragoons moved at a canter off the parade ground and rode towards the lines, seeing, as they quickened into a gallop, the lurid glare which stained the light of the moon, the gutted buildings and tottering walls. But there was no sign of the mutineers, who had done their work and were hurrying away from the vengeance which they knew would follow it. The long, disorderly column streamed down the Delhi road, the cavalry shouldering their dismounted fellows aside, the infantry stumbling over ditches and fields; all of them looking over their shoulders, the heat gone out of them and the chill of the coming reckoning settling down in its place: expecting every moment to hear the trumpets and see the flash of the guns behind them.

On the parade ground, the troops stood in their ranks. They had been marched back there, after the failure to save the lines, and again Hewitt waited and discussed and did nothing. The most that he would do was to detach a company or two for guard duty on the European lines, where, by this time, there was little left to guard. The red glow of the fires sank down, the moon waned, a cold breeze blew across the

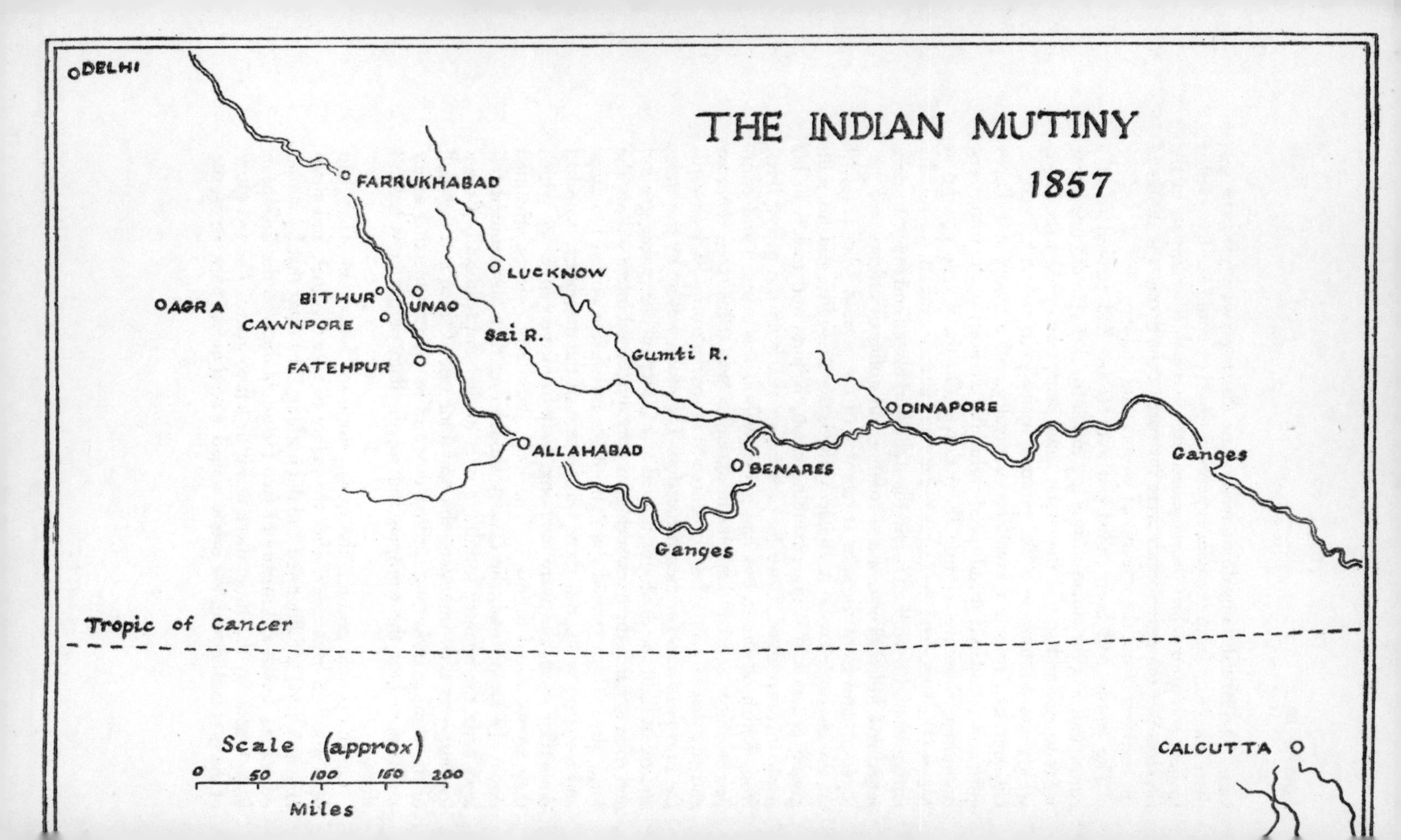
THE INDIAN MUTINY
1857
DELHI
FARRUKHABAD
LUCKNOW
AGRA
BITHUR
UNAO
CAWNPORE
Sai R.
FATEHPUR
Gumti R.
DINAPORE
ALLAHABAD
BENARES
Ganges
Ganges
Tropic of Cancer
Scale (approx)
0 50 100 150 200
Miles
CALCUTTA

ground where the troops still stood, till the light grew in the east and the sun rose on a scene of desolation. Far away, down the Delhi road, the mutineers, hearing no sound of pursuit, pressed on their way to join their fellows at the City of the Moguls, there to tell the story of their destruction of one of the most important military posts of India, of their escape unscathed, and of the utter powerlessness of the once feared Feringhees.

Delhi was now wholly in the hands of the mutineers—a strong place of defence and a rallying point for thousands who came from other scenes of mutiny. Willoughby and his men had wrecked the powder store and destroyed much of the arsenal, but not even an explosion of that size could destroy all in it that was valuable, and thousands of muskets and hundreds of guns fell into the hands of the mutineers. Day after day, new parties rode in, until the city was crowded with the offscourings of a dozen mutinies. Both Canning and Grant, who was acting as C.-in-C., decided that its reduction must be their first task, and every battalion and battery which could be spared was sent to join the investing force in its camp on the famous Ridge. Sir Harry Barnard was in command, Chamberlain and Baird Smith were with him and one day John Nicholson rode in with his escort of Pathans and a squadron of his Mooltan Horse—fierce little men on hill ponies, worshipping Nikkal-Seyn as their god. Among the Horse Artillery there was a subaltern called Roberts, who was to win the Victoria Cross and to live to command a British Army in the field.

It was a wise decision to concentrate on the capture of Delhi but, at the same time, there were posts which stood in even greater need and for the relief of which there were as yet no troops available. In Lucknow, Henry Lawrence, with the temporary rank of Brigadier-General, fortified the Residency and prepared to stand a siege. He was hopelessly outnumbered, but he held a strong position and he was well supplied with food and water. The garrison at Cawnpore were in more serious danger, nor was their commandant a man of Lawrence's calibre. Like Hewitt of Meerut, Sir Hugh Wheeler had spent a lifetime in the service in India, and he was now over seventy. He was both brave and competent, but he was worn out both physically and mentally, and he did not take precautions as quickly as did Lawrence at Lucknow. To some extent, he was hoodwinked—as Lawrence surely would not have been—by the apparent friendliness of the Nana Sahib, who overwhelmed him with offers of help. The Nana had waited for many years for this day of vengeance on the British.

When reports of outbreaks at other stations began to come into

Cawnpore, Wheeler bestirred himself to prepare a defensive position in case it should be needed. Those of his officers who had more knowledge of the principles of war tried to persuade him to fortify the magazine, which was a stout building, well adapted for defence and large enough to hold all the Europeans of the garrison with their families and where there was an ample supply of ammunition. But Wheeler felt—and it is hard to blame him, though many did at the time and have done since—that there might be safer positions than the top of a powder mine. In an unhappy moment he selected the building known as the Dragoons Hospital, at the moment disused, a building of little strength and tactically as bad as it could be. Here he ordered the construction of an entrenchment round the hospital, encircling a patch of bare ground with a wall of mud and prickly pear. He ordered supplies for twenty-five days to be stocked there, unwisely leaving the task to native contractors, who carried it out after the fashion of all native and many British contractors. 'The tangible result', Trevelyan comments, 'of a fortnight's labour and supervision, at a time when every hour was precious and every day priceless, consisted in a few cartloads of coarse native food, and a fence not high enough to keep out an active cow.'

The Nana Sahib observed these precautions with outward concern and inward amusement and tried to convince Wheeler of their uselessness. His own troops were ready and he was only too glad to lend them for the protection of the British, in the unlikely event of any trouble arising. Wheeler was deceived and accepted the Nana's kind offer with gratitude, offering him the duty of assuring the safety of the Treasury, a task which, as it happened, the Nana had been about to propose for himself. The troops from Bithur moved in and the Nana, the better to watch his devil's fun, took over a house in the cantonments for his own use. On 18th May Sir Hugh Wheeler telegraphed to the Government at Calcutta:

> 'All well at Cawnpore. Quiet, but excitement continues among the people. The final advance on Delhi will soon be made. . . . The plague is in truth stayed.'

His trustfulness and lack of ordinary precautions were to be the ruin of the garrison. It is only fair to record that, when that day came, Sir Hugh shared their sufferings and at last their death with fortitude and high courage. It was his misfortune to be placed at the end of a long and honourable life in a situation which called for a younger and more vigorous man.

The entrenchment was ready for occupation at the beginning of June, and by that time the situation of the garrison of Cawnpore had become precarious, as repeated mutinies in the province of Oudh cut their communications and threatened their reinforcement or relief. Benares and Allahabad were in mutiny, Fatehpur, on the main Cawnpore road, joined them, so that any relieving force would have to fight for many of the eighty miles which they had to march. On the 21st Wheeler decided that it was time to take to the entrenchment, and the women and children were sent in to occupy the hospital and any other shelter which they could find. The officers and the European troops remained at duty outside the entrenchment.

On the 22nd a small reinforcement of two officers and thirty-two other ranks marched in from Lucknow, where Lawrence, in the midst of his own troubles, had time and courage to remember the needs of another station. There was an uneasy time of waiting through the first days of July, while the Europeans went about their routine duties and the native troops muttered and conspired in their lines, while the women and children sweltered in the comfortless hospital and the barren entrenchment. On the 4th, the now familiar signs began with the burning of houses and the rattle of random musket shots, and Wheeler ordered the occupation of the entrenchment. If he had trusted the Nana, he was soon to be undeceived. The shallow pretence of friendship for the British was thrown aside and the Nana assumed the leadership of the mutineers. The troops and guns which he had brought into Cawnpore, ostensibly for the protection of the Treasury, were turned against the entrenchment. Late in the evening of that day the officers, who had stayed among their men until the last possible moment, went into the entrenchment and the siege began.

From the start the British were hopelessly outnumbered. There were 900 of them inside the fragile fortress, and, of these, 400 were women and children. Of the rest some 400 were Europeans and 100 were the loyal remnant of the garrison. Surrounding them were more than 3,000 fully armed and well-equipped natives. The British had one heavy howitzer and two field guns, while at first the enemy had fifteen guns, some of them of heavy calibre, and, as the siege went on, the number of them increased. The defensive position, which Wheeler had selected, could hardly have been more hopeless. The only protection was a breast-high wall made of mud, which crumbled in sun and melted in rain. The hospital was a building of no strength and quite inadequate for shelter, even of the women and children, and there was no shade anywhere else in the position; and this was at the height of an Indian summer, under the vertical rays of the sun and with a temperature which rose to 130 degrees. Worst of all, their only source of water was one well, in a position where it was commanded by the fire of the investing artillery. They had a poor supply of rations, both in quality and quantity, which would have been even worse were it not that the various messes had sent in generous supplies of beer, wine, spirits and delicacies.

The shelling began almost before the British had manned their posts, and they waited for the first attack but it did not come for several days. The mutineers had no taste for a hand-to-hand fight if they could achieve their object by the safer method of artillery fire, and, by day and night, they raked the entrenchment with round-shot and shells. The British casualties began to mount as the fire increased and as gun after gun was brought up to join in the bombardment. On the 12th the mutineers launched their first attack, but it wilted under the steady fire of the Enfield rifles and they turned and ran for shelter. There was no shelter for the beleaguered British, either against the incessant gunfire or the cruel sun. Next day they broke out of the entrenchment in force and fiercely attacked in their turn, killing and wounding many of the enemy and retracing their steps without serious loss. The action did much to raise their spirits and more to discourage the enemy from further assaults, but Wheeler and all the soldiers of the garrison knew how slight were their chances. The nearest help was at Lucknow, where Lawrence himself was besieged and there were no British troops nearer than Calcutta, except for a few isolated units who were fully occupied with the outbreaks in their own districts. They knew that the bulk of the army was attacking Delhi, but they did not know that a force for their relief was hastily being collected and that a small part of it was already on the move. Had they known, it would have been poor comfort, since what few troops were available were still near Calcutta and between them and Cawnpore were Benares and Allahabad, both held by mutinous native regiments. It seemed impossible for help to arrive in time.

CHAPTER XV

ALLAHABAD (1857)

LORD CANNING's harshest critics could not deny his courage in a crisis nor his ability to take quick and decided action in anything which did not involve judicial questions or nice points of conscience. He threw all his energy into the task of getting reinforcements for the hard-pressed troops and of relieving the beleaguered towns. He took the responsibility of stopping several troop-ships, which were on the way to China, and ordering them to turn into Indian ports and disembark the troops there. The units which were in Persia were sent back, most of them going straight to Calcutta, without calling at their home ports, and every battalion and battery which could be spared was sent up from Bombay and Madras, where the natives still showed no disposition to join in the mutiny.

One of the earliest units to arrive, and certainly one of the most efficient, was the 1st Madras Fusiliers, who had been in Persia with Outram and landed in Calcutta on 23rd May. The Fusiliers were one of the European regiments which were maintained by the East India Company and consisted largely of Irishmen. Their commanding officer was Colonel James Neill, who had served as a major in the Crimea and in Persia and had just taken over command of the regiment. They were assigned to the force which was being assembled for the relief of Cawnpore and Lucknow, and, as Neill was the senior officer available at the moment, he was given command of it.

So great was the urgency that he was ordered not to wait for the formation of the brigade, but to press on with his own regiment and a few details from other arms, which included some of the officers and men of a battery of artillery which had been summoned from Ceylon but had not brought its guns nor, as yet, acquired any more. The commanding officer was Captain Maude, an officer of exceptional merit, who was later to win the Victoria Cross and to write one of the most vivid memoirs of the Cawnpore campaign.

Neill was to march by way of Benares and Allahabad, at both of which stations the native troops had mutinied, and he was charged with the duty of suppressing and punishing the mutineers whom he would meet as he marched. It was a congenial task for the hard Scots Puritan believing, as he did, in his mission. History records few cruelties worse than those done by men who have honestly called themselves the servants of the God of Mercy.

In spite of transport difficulties and of obstruction by civilian officials, Neill pushed on to Benares, which he reached on 3rd June—the day on which, in Cawnpore, Wheeler had been forced to give up any idea of avoiding a mutiny and had ordered the manning of the entrenchments. Communications were so bad that no one knew exactly what was the position there, except that Wheeler had recently reported that there were signs of mutiny among the native troops. For all that Neill knew at the time of entering Benares, Lucknow might be in greater need than Cawnpore. He stopped long enough at Benares to disarm a disaffected native battalion and to turn the guns of a battery on to a battalion of Sikhs, who had, according to later evidence, no intention of mutinying, but had been alarmed into panic by the rumour that the British were about to attack them. Having taught Benares a lesson, he hurried on to Allahabad, where he was sorely needed. The 6th Native Infantry were in mutiny and had butchered their officers, together with a party of young cadets who had just arrived from England and were awaiting posting to their regiments. Neill burst upon the town too late to catch the mutineers, who had left after breaking open the gaol to release the prisoners and after plundering and killing in the streets. A detachment of Sikhs, under Captain Brayser, had remained true to their duty and joined Neill's force.

He arrived in Allahabad on the day on which the Nana's first assault was beaten off from the entrenchment at Cawnpore. Lord Canning, reporting to the Chairman of the Company, wrote:

> 'At Allahabad, the 6th regiment has mutinied, and fearful atrocities were committed by the people on Europeans outside the fort. But the fort has been saved. Colonel Neill, with nearly 300 European Fusiliers, is in it: and that point, the most precious in India at this moment, and for many years the most neglected, is safe, thank God. A column will collect there (with all speed which the means of conveyance will allow of) which Brigadier Havelock, just returned from Persia, will command.'

The unpleasing news of his supersession greeted Neill at Allahabad, where he was engaged in assembling the various units which continued to arrive to make up the force which was to relieve Cawnpore and Lucknow. He had not had long in which to enjoy his first independent command and there is a trace of acerbity in the letter in which he reports that, 'We are hard at work, collecting men and supplies for General Havelock's force.' But, wisely, he declined to remain inactive, while the necessary work was going forward, and sent his second-in-command, Major Renaud, with a wing of his regiment and a few guns, to push forward down the Cawnpore road, and another smaller force to cover their flank from a river steamer on the Ganges. Havelock arrived in Allahabad on 26th June and took over command from Neill. Their first meeting was perfectly friendly and Havelock spoke in warm and generous approval of the preparations which Neill had made and of his orders to Renaud. The orders included drastic rules for dealing with mutineers apprehended on the way and for their trial and execution in the most summary manner possible, and these too Havelock approved. He was as convinced as was Neill of the necessity of ruthless punishment and of inspiring terror in the countryside, though he never contemplated methods so wholesale and so cruel as Neill was to practise. Their greatest trouble was the lack of means for moving their men and guns, since all the bullocks in the neighbourhood had been destroyed or carried off by the mutineers, and foraging parties had to ride far and fast to bring in a few at a time wherever they could find them. Havelock and Neill chafed at the delay, believing that every day which they lost for this reason meant another day of anxiety and danger at Cawnpore.

But at Cawnpore it was all over—all except the vilest part of it. On the day on which Havelock rode into Allahabad, the garrison of the entrenchment had capitulated to the Nana Sahib, on the promise of fair terms and an honourable retreat. They had endured the hell of that entrenchment for three weeks, under the merciless Indian sun and under the incessant fire of the guns. They had beaten off two big assaults, made by ten times their own number, and they had lost more than half their own strength by sunstroke or shellfire. They were without ammunition, nearly without food, and what little water they could get was won daily at the cost of lives from the one well in the entrenchment on which the fire of the Nana's guns was concentrated. Wheeler and his officers would have tried one last sortie and broken out, to die, if need be, with their swords in their hands, rather than give in, but there were women and children in the garrison, and for their sake, whom the Nana promised to respect, they gave in at last.

On the next day, the 27th, as Havelock and Neill at Allahabad were planning their deliverance, the garrison, trusting the Nana's word, left their entrenchment and marched down to the river, carrying their sick and the very young in litters, to the boats which were to take them to Allahabad and safety. The Nana was at the riverside to see them go, and, hidden in bushes and behind walls all along one bank, were the Nana's riflemen, under Tantia Topee. As soon as the boats had pushed out into the stream the massacre began. There were forty boats, and only one got away from the destruction, carrying three officers and two privates as the sole survivors of the military garrison. The civilians were less fortunate, for the soldiers had died fighting, firing, as long as they could hold a rifle, at the murderers on the banks, plunging overboard and charging up the steeply sloping sand, to strike a dying blow with sword or bayonet. But the sick and wounded, the few men too old or too feeble to carry a gun, the women and the children, fell into the Nana's hands. The men were butchered on the instant before the eyes of the women, and the women and children were marched back to Cawnpore to await the Nana's pleasure. While the work of preparation went on at Allahabad, the women were imprisoned in a building near the Nana's house, fed on the coarsest native food, and compelled to do menial tasks for their captors. There were above two hundred of them and, by the Nana's mercy, they had still a few days to live. On 1st July the Nana proclaimed himself Peishwa of Bithur.

The story of the massacre reached Allahabad on 3rd July, as the preparations were drawing to a close. Neill refused to believe it, declaring it to be a rumour put out to mislead them in the hope that, since Cawnpore had fallen, they would turn their steps elsewhere, but Havelock did not doubt it. It was the first real difference between them, and Neill maintained his view with violence, urging that they should start at once, ready or not, since the garrison at Cawnpore were holding out and the enemy were spreading false information in the hope of gaining time. Havelock would have none of it. He knew that it was only too likely that the story was true. True or not, it would advantage nobody if his force set out so ill-equipped as to be unable to reach their destination. He reported the story to the Commander-in-Chief, adding that he was ready to march out as soon as he had equipped a force of 1,400 men: and adding too a generous appreciation of all the work which Neill had done before his arrival:

> 'Lieutenant-Colonel Neill, whose high qualities I cannot sufficiently praise, will follow with another column as soon as it can be organised,

> and this fort left in proper hands. I should have preferred to move the whole of our troops together, but the relief of Lucknow is an affair of time, and I cannot hazard its fall by waiting for the organisation of Neill's column.'

Havelock had set 7th July as the date for his departure from Allahabad. He no longer hoped to relieve Cawnpore, but he was determined to re-take it, both to inflict a blow on the enemy and to have it for an advanced base for his further move to Lucknow. He assigned to Neill the duty of holding down the districts of Benares and Allahabad, of collecting and assembling reinforcements as they came in and of sending them forward as quickly as possible. Finally, when the whole force had arrived, Neill was to follow with the last contingent.

It is likely that Neill felt aggrieved at being relegated to this secondary role, and it is certain that from this time onwards the relations between the two men rapidly deteriorated. For this Neill was wholly to blame, for his conduct was indefensible by any standards of military decency. He had, unknown to Havelock, already taken it upon himself to telegraph to the acting C.in-C., Sir Patrick Grant, alleging that the story of the fall of Cawnpore was a pure fabrication and complaining of Havelock's delay in starting. He continued to write in this disloyal way at intervals, not hesitating to criticise his superior. Apart from the disloyalty of it, Neill surely ought to have reflected that Havelock was an experienced officer, who had commanded a division in action, while he himself had only just succeeded to command of a battalion, and that it was just possible that Havelock knew more about his job than he did. He was putting Grant, too, in an intolerable position, for they were friends of long standing, and Grant had enough to do without having to attend to an unauthorised and ill-tempered correspondent. He was on the point of giving up his own appointment as acting C.-in-C. and was preparing to join the army in front of Delhi as soon as Sir Colin Campbell should have arrived to take over from him. He was therefore hardly in a position to reply to Neill either as a friend or, officially, as C.-in-C. Later, when Campbell had arrived, Grant wrote to Neill, who had become more pressing and more outspoken about his superior officer, a letter of gentle rebuke and advice;

> 'I do not write to you as your Commander in Chief, but as your friend, and in that capacity would beg of you to get on smoothly with your immediate superiors and not allow differences to arise between you. You are too old a soldier not to be aware that, if the senior officers of a force in the field get to loggerheads, the public service must inevitably suffer; and I know you and Havelock too well not to feel that such a result would be infinitely painful to both of you.'

It would certainly have been made painful to Neill, if Havelock had at this time had any idea that he was acting with such disloyalty, but Havelock was absorbed in getting his force ready to advance. In nearly every way, it was as ill-equipped and ill-found as it could have been, and, considering what task it was to undertake, it was hopelessly inadequate in numbers as well as in equipment.

Eighty miles separate Allahabad from Cawnpore and another forty separate Cawnpore from Lucknow, and they might have to fight several engagements on their way to either place or both places. The enemy's strength was unknown, but there were certainly not less than 3,500 Sepoys at Cawnpore and more were arriving every day. The Gwalior contingent were not yet known to be in mutiny, but it was taken for granted that any day they might arrive to swell the numbers to double that figure, and from Lucknow itself the enemy could easily despatch a force of equal size to destroy any attempt at relief, while they contained the garrison. Seldom had a British brigade been asked to take such a leap into the unknown—never probably a brigade so small and so ill-found for their task.

Major Renaud of the Madras Fusiliers, who was on the Cawnpore Road, ahead of the main body, had with him 400 European infantry of his own regiment and the 84th Foot and 300 of Brayser's Sikhs, supported by a few native irregular cavalry and two 9-pounder guns. The main body which marched out under Havelock consisted of less than a thousand British infantry, drawn from the Madras Fusiliers, the 64th and 84th Foot and the 78th Highlanders. They had eighteen cavalrymen, mostly officers from regiments which had been disbanded, though a few of them were civilians. The artillery had an experienced commandant in Captain Maude, but they had very little else. Their guns had been hastily drawn from the store in Allahabad, and they had not been able to find horses to draw them, so that the gun teams were composed of oxen. They were so short of gunners that they had had to take volunteers from the infantry and give them hasty and superficial intruction in gun-drill. The one advantage which the Fusiliers possessed was that they were all armed with the Enfield rifle. In every other respect, their equipment was useless or unsuitable. The infantry, many of whom had arrived straight from the winter campaign in Persia, were still wearing the heavy woollen clothing in which they had fought there. There were no supplies of tropical clothing and no time to wait for them and all that they could improvise for a campaign in the height of the Indian midsummer was an inadequate supply of white linen cap-covers, made after the fashion of the early Crusades, with a flap at the back to protect the neck from the sun. Horses were hardly to be had anywhere in the district and those officers who had been lucky enough to find one had only too often paid a huge price for a totally useless charger. There was a shortage of wheeled transport, of medical supplies and of food and the barest necessaries, and they soon found that there was no hope of supplying themselves, as they marched, from the surrounding countryside, from which all stock had been driven off, and everything else burnt or taken by Renaud's advance guard. It was a naked force advancing into a naked country, and no one knew it better than their Brigadier, as he sat on his horse at the Cawnpore gate of Allahabad and grimly watched them march out. Maude, who rode ahead of his gunners, left a vivid description of the slight figure which sat so upright in the saddle of the arab charger. Havelock's hair was perfectly white, but he was as erect as ever. He wore, as he continued to wear throughout the campaign, a blue frock-coat, tan leggings which were buttoned from thigh to ankle, and a forage cap with white cover. His Adjutant-General, Captain Stuart Beatson, and his Quartermaster-General, Lieutenant-Colonel Fraser Tytler, were on their horses behind him and his son, Henry, of the 10th Foot, was with him, as A.D.C.

They marched at half-past four in the afternoon in a storm of rain which soaked their heavy clothing and added to its weight, and which turned the dust of the roads to clinging mud, so that men could hardly raise their feet and the oxen slipped and fell as they strained in the traces of the guns. An officer who marched with them noticed that, as they left the gate, the native people came to the doors of their houses with gestures of hatred but without sound. It was unwise to raise a shout while Neill remained in the town, where the gibbets of his Provost-Major were beginning to rise like a forest.

> 'Ploughing through the slush and drenched by the rain [so Sir William Hunter describes their going] the soldiers, as they left the city behind, saw in front and on either side a vast and dreary waste dotted with the charred ruins of forsaken villages. Not a living man was to be seen: only here and there some loathsome swine, gnawing the flesh from a dead body. It seemed as though the destroying angel had passed over the land.'

CHAPTER XVI

FATEHPUR (1857)

THE COLUMN had started in the afternoon, and when they halted for the night, just before midnight, they had only accomplished a march of six miles. The guns were far behind where the oxen had become bogged down in the mud, while their sweating drivers and the gunners toiled with spade and crowbar, with shoulders to wheels and with extra traces, to drag them out of the quagmire. The waggons with the tents had shared the same fate and the few horses of the cavalry had all but foundered. The brigade settled into their bivouacs on that cheerless plain without shelter or food, other than a few biscuits, while the pitiless rain drove at them and the mud threatened to engulf them where they lay.

Havelock slept as best he could on the ground among them, with his cloak for his only covering. The days when the transport's first duty was to carry the comforts of the general and staff were gone, and staff and regimental officers fared no otherwise than did their men. Havelock, when he awoke in the grey and rainy dawn, must have remembered that he was sixty-two and found that his bones ached as they had not ached on the way to Kabul. The brigade awoke to the same sight of a desolate plain, of pouring rain, to the feeling of sodden clothes and empty bellies. For three more days the rain and the mud held them and they made no more than eight or nine miles a day. Havelock must have fretted at the delay, but he would not press them too much at the start, until the recruits had found their feet and the trained soldiers had recovered theirs. In the comparative comfort of Allahabad, Neill fumed at their slowness as the messages came back, but Havelock held on at his steady pace, keeping his troops closed up and allowing the guns to keep pace with them. Neill was impatient because he believed that Cawnpore was untaken and that there would still be time to relieve the garrison. He had passed this opinion on to

Sir Patrick Grant, who shared it and began to urge Havelock forward. Renaud was out in front with less than a battalion's strength and, if the gap between the two forces were too great, Renaud might easily be overwhelmed before Havelock could help him. Havelock knew all this. He would put on all possible speed but he would not wreck his brigade by overdriving them before they had come into contact with the enemy.

From every military point of view he was right, for he did not yet know the worst of the news—that, while all the men of the garrison had perished, there were still over 200 women and children in the Nana's prison, held there either as possible hostages or for an ultimate act of vengeance. As far as Havelock knew, the whole garrison had been destroyed and his business at Cawnpore would be punishment and not deliverance. His destination thereafter would be Lucknow and, on the day that he left Allahabad, he had heard from Henry Lawrence that he could hold out for a month without difficulty. It was then the merest act of prudence to handle his force with husbandry, knowing that at any time he would have to demand from them a tremendous effort in face of overwhelming superiority of numbers.

As they toiled over the plain on the 8th, 9th and 10th, there were already signs that the pace at which Renaud had moved had overtaxed even his well-trained Fusiliers. They came upon men who had fallen beside the rough track and died there from exposure, from sunstroke, from exhaustion, and across men who still lived but lacked the strength to drag their exhausted bodies any further. Soon there were even grimmer tokens of Renaud's passing in the gibbets, each with its putrifying burden, which stood by the roadside, sometimes singly or in pairs, sometimes like a small plantation. Renaud had liberally interpreted the disciplinary rules which Neill had given him and which Havelock had approved. He had thoroughly put into effect the *Code Neill*, which was for a time to supersede the traditional methods of British justice.

It was an expeditious code; necessarily so, because the court sat while the regiment marched and did not care to be left too far behind in a nice scrutiny of evidence. Nor was much evidence necessary, since any native was assumed to be a mutineer, unless he could prove the contrary, always a difficult task in the absence of witnesses or counsel for the accused. Since the court was summary, no time need be wasted on appeal or on confirmation of sentence, and the only punishment was death, which was dealt out on the spot, while the court mounted and rode on to their next appointment.

On the 11th Havelock began to force the pace a little more. He was beginning to feel anxious about the safety of Renaud's contingent and the improvement in the weather made it possible to pull the guns faster as they came to harder ground. They made fifteen miles before they stopped for the night and Havelock gave the order to be ready to march again at midnight. His medical officers tried to dissuade him, urging that the men were completely exhausted, but he refused to listen. He could be as ruthless in case of need as he was reasonable when there was no urgency, and he knew now that time was short. Colonel Tytler, his D.A.Q.M.G., included among his duties those which nowadays would be carried out by the Intelligence, and Havelock, as the result of many years of experience in the East, put his trust in spies whom he rewarded generously out of the funds which were put at the Army's disposal for such purposes. He had always found that a combination of cupidity and fear would induce the native to risk his life in a spying enterprise and to tell something approximating to the truth in his report. That no native ever told the truth if he could help it Havelock well knew, but he and Tytler were practised in disentangling the gist of a confused and exaggerated tale. The spies knew that if their information was good they would be generously paid, and that if it proved to be false they would be promptly hanged. They came in now to report that Renaud was only a few miles in front, and that only a few more miles further on a force of over 3,000 of the enemy were advancing to attack him, believing his force to be alone and unsupported by any main body.

The mutineers were accompanied by the guns which they had looted from the magazine at Cawnpore and they were supported by a mass of irregular levies, followers of the Nana Sahib, many of whom were mounted. Renaud had with him 400 British and 300 Sikhs, with two light guns and no cavalry. Havelock realised at once that he must either order him to withdraw on to the main body or else hurry to his support, and he decided against ordering any withdrawal. It would have a depressing effect on the morale of his own and of Renaud's troops and would give the enemy encouragement which they would be better without. Above all he was anxious to conceal the presence of the main body from the enemy until the fire of its guns should announce it from a position of his own choice, and he would not risk a pursuit of Renaud by the enemy's cavalry, who were numerous and well-mounted and might overtake them and get wind of the support on to which they would be retiring. He overruled the doctors and the brigade marched at midnight. An hour later they overtook Renaud and the combined forces continued their march through the early hours of the morning of the 12th. About seven o'clock in the morning they halted and began to prepare their breakfast.

The troops were tired out and Havelock had intended to give them the whole day for rest, but the enemy were nearer than his spies had led him to think. Unlike many of the senior officers under whom he had served, he was meticulous about reconnaissance, and while the men flung themselves on the ground or began to coax the little fires into life, Tytler and a scouting party rode ahead. They had not ridden far towards the small town of Fatehpur, which lay just ahead of them, when the enemy opened fire with a 24-pounder gun, the shot of which flew over their heads and ended up near to the spot in the camp where Havelock was standing. The bugles sounded the alarm and the men threw down stew-pot and kettle and snatched up rifle and bayonet, as Tytler and his party galloped into the camp. Behind them there was the noise of shouts and of horses' hoofs, as the enemy's cavalry covered the plain in pursuit of what they took to be an isolated unit of no strength. Havelock gave his orders swiftly, and the British moved into position as the enemy cavalry wheeled away to the flank and revealed their main body in front of the town. 'It was a place of no small strength', in Havelock's own words.

> 'The hard and dry trunk road subdivides it and is the only means of convenient access, for the plains on both sides are covered at this season by heavy lodgements of water, to the depth of two, three and four feet. It is surrounded by garden enclosures of great strength, with high walls and has within it many houses of good masonry. In front of the swamps are hillocks, villages and mango groves, which the enemy already occupied in force.'

It was in fact just such a neat little defensive position as had proved irresistible in the past to such commanders as Gough and Hardinge, presenting an opportunity for a determined frontal attack with the bayonet at a probable cost of a few hundred casualties. The flanks were protected by floods and the front by walls and gardens in which an assaulting infantry would find themselves entangled and obstructed under the fire of heavy guns.

Henry Havelock, as he watched his infantry deploy and Maude's guns wheel into line for the first fight in which he had held an independent command, was looking back into the past, but beyond Sobraon and Ferozepore: back to a subaltern's study in the barracks at Shorncliffe, and again, beyond that, to the words of one of the great captains of history, who laid down the principle, 'Le feu est tout: le reste est peu-de-chose.' He had no more intention than would the Emperor Napoleon have had of walking into a cross fire and he had in the Enfield rifle a tactical weapon which Gough never knew. He had the advantage of surprise on his side, since the enemy probably still believed that all that faced them was Renaud's weak force.

Since they would be watching his centre, he stripped it of all but Maude's battery with 100 men of the 64th for local protection, while his infantry swiftly deployed to right and left. Renaud's Fusiliers, on the extreme right, brushed an advanced post of the enemy off a hillock which they occupied, while Colonel Hamilton's 78th on their left linked them with the battery in the centre. Brayser's Sikhs took the extreme left with the small party of the 84th, under Lieutenant Ayrton on their right, linked on that side to the centre by the remainder of Major Stirling's 64th. Skirmishers covered the deployment and the tiny bodies of irregular and volunteer cavalry moved out to support each flank.

The enemy calmly awaited the first attack on the centre, which never came. In their own centre were the 56th Native Infantry, whom Havelock had had under his command at Maharajapore. The mutineers fought for the most part in the full uniform which they had disgraced and sometimes carried the colours which they had deserted, and it was not difficult to pick them out when it was known what regiments had mutinied and where they had gone. As Havelock stood watching the deployment, one of his staff who stood beside him saw him gazing through his glass at the 56th and heard him growl, 'There's some of you there that have seen me fighting. Now try on yourselves what you've seen me do.'

The Enfield rifles opened fire all along the front and the bullets whipped into the enemy at a range far beyond anything that they had thought of, and with an accuracy and a rapidity of fire of which their smooth-bored muskets were quite incapable. The Madras Fusiliers had the name of being the best marksmen in India, and, from their position on the hillock, they could enfilade a good part of the enemy's line.

The Sepoys were confounded by this sudden torrent of fire, to which they could not reply because of the length of the range, and, while they were hesitating, Maude and his gunners manhandled their guns down the slope till they were almost within point-blank range of the Sepoys' advanced line. Their first salvo blasted the centre of it and the Sepoys turned and ran.

If Havelock had had just one regiment of cavalry, he could have driven the enemy in headlong rout and inflicted heavy damage on them. His little handful of horsemen trotted forward, the volunteers with enthusiasm, the native irregulars with unconcealed distaste. The horses were tired out and could hardly raise a canter, but Palliser, leading the irregulars, managed to overtake the retreating enemy and called on his men for a charge. Only a few of them followed him and he nearly lost his life among the horde of native horsemen, from whom he was saved by the bravery of his native Rissaldar. Havelock had to suffer the mortification of a victorious general who sees a beaten enemy retreating and lacks the means to turn the retreat into a rout.

The brigade lay down to sleep that night triumphant but utterly exhausted. They had marched twenty-four miles and fought an action and neither man nor beast could move a step further. Havelock had already decided to allow them at least twenty-four hours' complete rest, and all day on the 13th they lay in their bivouacs, except for the necessary sentries, and slept and ate and slept again. There was no sleep for Havelock once the night had passed, for urgent matters of discipline needed his attention. He dealt sharply with the irregular cavalry, in punishment for their cowardice, depriving them of their arms and their horses and relegating them to fatigues and carrying of baggage. The volunteers gladly took the horses for their own use, having for a long time coveted them. In the confusion of the rapid arming at Allahabad the worthless irregulars had been allowed to take valuable horses from a Government stud near the town, while the volunteers had had to content themselves with such country hacks as they had been able to get from dealers, often at an exorbitant price.

During the day Havelock published his order to his troops which was soon to become famous. He had been a lifelong admirer of Napoleon and something of that magniloquent French style is reflected in its opening, recalling the 'Officiers! Sous-Officiers! Soldats!' of the great days of the Grande Armée.

> 'General Havelock thanks his soldiers for their arduous exertions of yesterday, which produced in four hours the strange result of a rebel army driven from a strong position, eleven guns captured, and their whole force scattered to the winds without the loss of a single British soldier. To what is this astounding effect to be attributed? To the fire of British Artillery, exceeding in rapidity and precision all that the Brigadier has ever witnessed in his not short career; to the power of the Enfield rifle in British hands; to British pluck, that great quality which has survived the vicissitudes of the hour and gained intensity from the crisis; and to the blessing of Almighty

God on a most righteous cause, the cause of humanity, justice, truth and good government in India.'

Some contemporaries, who did not know Havelock, smiled at the respective places alloted to the Artillery, the Enfield rifle and Almighty God, but General Havelock, like General Cromwell, trusted in God and kept his powder dry. In a private letter to his wife he gave free expression to his personal happiness in the success of his first action as an independent commander, though he ended with the characteristic note of humility, 'But away with vainglory. Thanks to Almighty God, who gave me the victory.'

The Brigade still lay outside the town of Fatehpur and, now that he had disciplined his irregular cavalry, a grimmer act of justice had to be done on the town itself. A few weeks earlier the townspeople had risen in revolt and murdered Europeans, including Robert Tucker, the British Collector. Sherer, who had been Resident Magistrate, had escaped with his life and now rode with Havelock's staff, ready to reinstate British civil justice when the army had done their work. The people of the town had fled when the brigade was approaching and Havelock decided to give the town up to pillage by his troops. It was to be a ruthless act of justice and a warning to other towns which might be thinking of throwing up their allegiance to the Raj.

CHAPTER XVII

THE MASSACRE AT CAWNPORE (1857)

THERE IS no doubt that, as the campaign went on and anxiety was piled on anxiety, Havelock grew more unapproachable and more exacting, less ready to make allowances for human frailty, more apt to say things which were remembered afterwards. He had been given a task which was almost beyond human capability and he demanded almost more than human strength and endurance from his subordinates. He was a devout man, who firmly believed that he was engaged on God's work, and any weakness in others which delayed or impaired the work was an offence not against him, not against military discipline, but against God. He demanded the utmost from himself and from his officers and men, ignoring the fact that they might not have the same power of endurance or the same high sense of their mission.

The physical conditions of the campaign must have tried his strength sorely, since he was sixty-two and probably the oldest man in the Brigade. He shared all the discomforts of his men, sleeping on the bare ground, once at least with his saddled horse beside him and its bridle wrapped round his wrist, eating the same coarse and scanty food, soaked by the same rain, oppressed by the same heat. It was hard enough for the junior officers and men, most of whom were young or in the prime of life, and who did not have to bear the load of responsibility and the burden of decision which lay on his shoulders. It is little to be wondered at that, when at last the task was finished and Lucknow gained, he should quickly sink into weariness and ill-health and soon afterwards into death. His determination and courage had held him up while there was still work to do, but once his responsibility had passed to Outram and Inglis the burden which he had carried broke him in the moment of laying it down.

His anxieties were incessant during the next days when the army pressed on to Cawnpore. He had beaten the mutineers in battle, but their almost undiminished strength still lay between him and his first objective and, while their numbers were constantly being increased by fresh mutinies and desertions, his own were dwindling daily as men fell exhausted by heat or dead from sunstroke, and he did not know how soon or from whence he might expect help or reinforcement.

On the day after the fight at Fatehpur, a sharp new anxiety fell upon him, when his spies brought in a story that there were still British women and children in the Nana's hands at Cawnpore. He had no means of confirming the story which he hardly dared to believe, so dreadful might be their fate. Unlike Neill, he did not refuse to believe a report which did not suit him and he faced the fact that these British women and their children lay in deadly danger, while a huge force of the enemy interposed between them and the deliverance which he alone could bring. He knew the native mind and the Nana's reputation well enough to know how slender was their hope. That early morning, as the men fell in for the day's march, he cantered up to them to give them the news which, he well knew, would drive them to call up the last ounce of power and endurance which they had left.

The infantry, shuffling into their places in column, sore and aching after their exertions and with nothing to look forward to but another day of marching under a broiling sun, saw him approach without enthusiasm, fearing that he was about to make a speech to them. He had addressed them at some length before their departure from Allahabad, as those Roman generals, of whom he had read at Charterhouse, had been used to address their troops before action, and his 'contio' had not been well received, especially by the 78th Highlanders. The 64th and the gunners had raised a feeble cheer, but the Highlanders, suspicious of all Sassenach oratory, had remained sullenly mute, till Havelock, with quick tact, had called out to them, 'All right, 78th, I know you. You will cheer fast enough when you see the enemy in front of you.' That had pleased them and they cheered him lustily.

There was no cheering today and no 'contio'. Havelock knew that the news which he had to tell them would stir them far more than any words of his own, and he pulled up in front of them and said, 'Men, there are still women and children of our race in the hands of those fiends. By God's help, we will save them, or every man of us will die in the attempt.' A low growl, like that of wild beasts aroused, ran through the ranks, and they shouldered their rifles and moved off at a quick step. There would be no need for their officers to urge them to greater speed today. Even the Sikhs looked cheerful, though they had understood little of what he had said, and were not overmuch moved by the plight of the prisoners in Cawnpore. They had spent a pleasant day in plundering Fatehpur, and, as soon as the column had passed through it, they were to have the congenial task of burning it to the ground. Havelock Sahib had told them that they would soon be in Cawnpore, a rich city, in which they promised themselves such a time as they had not had since the meddlesome Neill Sahib had put an end to their fun in Allahabad. The liquor stores there had been full and the British throats dry, when they arrived to find the Sikhs in possession of all the stock of liquor in the town. Their religion forbade them to taste fermented liquors, but there was no law against selling them to the infidel, and they had done a roaring trade in champagne at a shilling and brandy at two shillings a bottle, until Neill Sahib had put his foot down and ordered the Commissariat to buy up all the stock. Perhaps Havelock Sahib would be more reasonable at Cawnpore.

Their British comrades could have disillusioned them, but even they would have been the happier could they have seen the indent for supplies and equipment which Havelock had just sent back to Neill. Among the indents for ammunition, tropical clothing, shrapnel and horses, was a request for rum. Havelock had never varied in his belief that 'the pure element' was the best drink for troops on service, but he was wise enough to know that exhausted men could whip themselves into renewed life, if only for a short while, after a ration of spirit, and that the rum would put warmth and heart into bodies weary with marching and drenched with rain.

After they had marched a few miles, Havelock pulled his horse out of the column and trotted back to the place where Maude rode ahead of his battery. Maude's memoir of the campaign is one of the liveliest and most vivid accounts and one from which it is possible to learn something of Havelock in his less formal moments. Havelock had soon seen that Maude knew his business thoroughly and had been impressed with his ingenuity in improvising transport for his guns as well as by the brilliant way in which he had fought them at Fatehpur. He treated him with more confidence and less restraint than he used to most of the other officers, and Maude on his side was pleased and perhaps a little flattered by the deep interest which Havelock seemed to take in the details of gunnery. As a staff-officer and a commander, Havelock had always been well-informed in the tactical use of artillery, but now he seemed anxious to learn the technical side. It may be that, having adopted his master's principle 'Le feu est tout', he had decided that he ought to know as much as he could about the subject, or simply that, at sixty-two, he was still a student of war and all information was welcome to him. That morning he asked Maude how long it would take him to bring one gun into action against a given target, to which Maude had replied with an estimate of one minute, eliciting a promise from Havelock that he would time the movement next time there was an opportunity.

The importance of exact timing became known as one of Havelock's idiosyncracies on that march to Cawnpore. Whenever they deployed for action, he would take his watch from his pocket and hand it to Dick Pearson, the bugler from the 78th, who was his orderly throughout the march, bidding him to mark exactly the time which elapsed between the beginning and end of a fight. The bugler told his comrades that on one occasion, as soon as the fight ended, he handed the watch back to its owner with the remark, 'Just two hours and forty-five minutes, sir.'

It is not quite clear what was the importance which Havelock attached to this matter of timing an action, but he was the most scientific of soldiers and there must have been an idea at the back of his mind about it. Even when writing to his wife, as he continued regularly to do, he never failed to mention the time which it had taken to carry out a movement or to win an action. Quite soon he was to have an opportunity of checking Maude's accuracy.

The brigade had marched long before dawn, and almost as soon as the sun was up their scouts reported that the enemy were in position round a little village called Aong. They did not appear to be strong in infantry but they had with them a large body of cavalry, so Havelock divided his force into two, giving Tytler about a third of them, with the task of dislodging the Sepoy infantry from their position while he himself kept the rest in hand to watch the cavalry, who were threatening his flanks and his baggage column, which marched in the rear. Tytler sent the Madras Fusiliers against the position at Aong, which they cleared without much difficulty, though it cost the life of Major Renaud, who was leading them. The enemy cavalry still threatened the flanks of the main body, but the guns and the Enfield rifles were too accurate for their comfort and they did not venture to push home an attack. It gave Havelock his opportunity to test Maude's estimate of one minute for bringing a gun into action and he found—doubtless to his satisfaction—that the movement had taken one and a half. Maude records that Havelock, riding up beside him again, twitted him with it and was told that there had been a delay in lighting a port-fire. (In enemy country the battery marched always with slow-matches burning, so that at any moment they could light the port-fires, the torches which were used for the actual firing of the guns.) Havelock told him gravely that he ought to march with his port-fires always burning. Maude, an officer of tact and experience, as gravely agreed, concealing the knowledge that to do so would exhaust his whole stock of port-fires in about forty-eight hours.

The brigade had marched for five hours and had stopped to eat their breakfast when they learned that the enemy were once more in position a few miles ahead at a stream called the Pandu Nuddhi. In a normal summer it would have been a mere trickle, easily fordable at a dozen places, but the heavy rains had swollen it into a raging torrent, which could only be crossed by the masonry bridge, round which the enemy had taken up their position. Havelock would gladly have given his men a longer rest but he realised the delay which would arise if the enemy were to blow up the bridge. He had no pontoon equipment and it would be impossible to find boats in that hostile country, so there was nothing for it but to push on as fast as possible and fight for possession of the bridge. The men, thinking of those women and children in Cawnpore, responded willingly and they marched at a good pace for another two hours. The enemy had a strong position on both banks of the Nuddhi, and had already prepared trenches for the defence of the bridge. Their guns were in position and among them were two 24-pounders, so placed as to sweep the approach to the bridge and the trunk road for 2,000 yards on the British side. It was a position which would have entailed heavy losses in any attempt at a frontal attack, but Havelock was no lover of frontal attacks. He had seen too many of them in Gwalior and the country near the Sutlej. He had no intention of obliging the enemy by walking into the trap which had been prepared for him. Once again Napoleon's maxim came back to him—'Le feu est tout'—and he sent for Maude who suggested a division of his battery so as to envelop the bridge with fire from both front and flanks. Havelock assented and quickly gave his orders, and three of Maude's guns turned off to each flank while the remaining two sought a covered position in front of the bridge. The tiny body of British cavalry made a demonstration of moving against the centre and the Madras Fusiliers, chosen as being the best marksmen in the brigade, worked their way through ravines which protected each flank, till they were forward and wide of the guns and could enfilade the enemy with their rifles.

The Sepoys trusted in their strong position and were misled by the feint of the cavalry. As they had done before, and as they were to do again, they seemed to discount any idea of a turning movement by the British, and they were taken unawares by the storm of shrapnel from the guns and the cross fire of the Enfields. For a moment Havelock must have known a sickening drop of the heart when a cloud of white smoke rose from the far side of the bridge and the dull sound of an explosion reached him, but the Sepoys had bungled their work of destruction, and a moment later Major Stephenson, who had succeeded Renaud in command of the Fusiliers, broke out of the woods with the right wing of his regiment and stormed across the undamaged bridge. The enemy fled precipitately as the 64th and the Highlanders charged down the slope in support of the Fusiliers.

The bridge was won and the last natural barrier between the British and Cawnpore had been passed. But the brigade could do no more. They had marched for seven hours and had fought two actions, though both combined had cost them no more than twenty-five casualties in killed and wounded. They still had twenty-two miles to go to reach their objective and they would almost certainly have to fight again before reaching it. No force on earth could have gone on farther without rest, and without food, since they had barely had time to snatch a mouthful at breakfast. They lay where they had halted with their arms beside them, too weary even to think of food until they had slept; and, while they slept, Sepoy horsemen galloped back along the trunk road to bring the news to the Nana Sahib at Cawnpore.

The Nana was wild with terror and rage, the more so that the Sepoys, who had soon tired of the authority of a commander who kept aloof from any of the fighting, jeered at him and seemed disposed to throw off the last vestiges of their allegiance. Against his will he was forced to order a march by all the available troops in Cawnpore to stem the tide of the British advance, and, even more against it, to promise to accompany the army, which was to be commanded by Tantia Topee.

Before he set out, he had more congenial work to do. He decided—possibly in the hope of removing evidence against himself—on the murder of all the prisoners who remained in his hands.

The few men among them were brought before him and shot then and there by a firing party of Sepoys. The women, with their children, were shut up in a building near the house which the Nana had occupied since the beginning of the siege and, towards evening, a native woman, who pitied them, went to the building and warned them of their danger. In desperation some of them must have torn their clothes and tried with the strips of linen and cloth to weave ropes to keep shut the door, for the British, when they arrived, found the slashed remnants of them hanging there.

There are some crimes so devilish that even a generation which has known wholesale destruction on the scale made common by two world wars must shudder on reading of them; so devilish, too, that even hardened criminals shrink from having a hand in them. The Sepoys, who had not scrupled to shoot the men, could not bring themselves to commit the final infamy. They fired a volley through the windows of the building, aiming so high that the shots passed over the heads of the prisoners. The marks of the bullets were there, to be plainly seen by Havelock's men, three days later. The Nana would not be denied his vengeance and, late in the evening, five men armed with knives went into the building. One was wearing Sepoy's scarlet, two were butchers from the bazaar. They were a long time in there and twice one of them came out to throw away a broken knife and to return with a fresh one. It was pitch dark when at last they all came out for the last time, but the sentries on the Nana's house heard groans and sobs coming from the slaughter-house all night, till in the early dawn men went in, and the dead and dying were thrown into the well in the courtyard. One of them told of the ultimate horror of little children, wounded but still able to move, who tried to escape from their murderers and were chased round the well, to be thrown, still breathing, into the depths with the rest.

Then it was full day and the Nana reluctantly went out with his retinue to make a last stand in front of Cawnpore.

There were over five thousand in the force which marched out of the town and took the trunk road towards the village of Maharajapore. They were strong in cavalry and had guns of all calibres from 24 to 9 pounds. The Nana went with them, riding in a gorgeous party, borne by elephants and surrounded by mounted men. Tantia Topee, who commanded and had learned from British officers some considerable skill, had chosen their position, which lay across the junction of two roads at a point where the road to the cantonment of Cawnpore joined the Grand Trunk to Delhi. Their left was protected by the River Ganges about a mile away and by the high ground which sloped down to it, where their heaviest guns were placed. Their right rested on the railway embankment and was covered by a village and by some mango groves, while their centre, a little retired, was some 800 yards short of the road junction. In the centre guns were massed so as to sweep the road junction and deny the use of either road to an advancing force. A mass of infantry supported the guns, and the cavalry, including the whole of the mutinous 2nd Native Horse, was in reserve behind them. It was a tremendously strong position, provided that the enemy could be relied on to use orthodox methods of attack. Tantia Topee, who had learned his tactics in an orthodox school, counted on a frontal attack with the bayonet. He did not yet know the deadly fire of the Enfield nor the fertile genius of the commander who opposed him.

The army of Cawnpore were astir after a wretched night of broken sleep, in pouring rain, against which they had no protection, and after such scraps of food as they had managed to find. The Commissariat had broken down as usual, but, as it happened, there was plenty of porter up with them, and Havelock had ordered the issue of a generous ration. Some of the recruits of the Madras Fusiliers, unused to strong drink on an empty stomach, were reeling as they fell in, but the older soldiers found it about as stimulating as milk and water and grumbled vigorously because the rum had not arrived. They moved on for a short distance and halted again. Then an order went round the waiting battalions and the men watched their commanding officers mount and ride up a slight slope, to a clump of trees where the Brigadier waited for them. When they reached the clump, they saw that he had dismounted and that his orderly bugler was leading his Arab horse up and down. The Brigadier was wearing the blue frock-coat and the white cap which they had seen so often during the past days, and his tan leggings were neatly buttoned from thigh to ankle. He had taken his sword out of its sling and was tracing designs on the bare ground with the end of the scabbard.

CHAPTER
XVIII
CAWNPORE RECAPTURED (1857)

THEY DISMOUNTED, handed their horses over to orderlies and walked to where the Brigadier was standing. He acknowledged their salutes a little absent-mindedly, but they were used to his ways now and knew that that look of abstraction hid a mind which was working with speed and precision. They were a little startled by his opening remark: 'Gentlemen, we are now about to repeat the manœuvre of the great Frederick at Leuthen.'

He went on to detail his plan with something of the precision of a sixth-form master instructing his form in Tacitus or Thucydides. He knew that, by choosing to stand on the defensive, Tantia Topee had thrown away his best chance of victory. If he had attacked boldly his huge preponderance in numbers would almost certainly have enabled him to hold the British with his infantry, while his cavalry swept round their flanks and enveloped them. Tantia had based his defence on the belief that Havelock would advance straight down the line of the trunk road and try to debouch towards the road which led to the cantonments, so coming under the direct fire of the massed guns in the Sepoy centre.

It was, of course, the last thing which Havelock had any intention of attempting. A turning movement had served him well in the past few days and he had as yet seen no disposition on the enemy's part to guard against a repetition of such a manœuvre. In his precise, almost pedantic way, and with the help of his tracery on the ground, he unrolled before his officers a plan so little pedantic that it went clean against every accepted principle of tactics. He proposed, contrary to all text-book maxims, to change front to a flank in face of the enemy, and move the whole of his guns and infantry to his right to turn the enemy's flank. It was a bold, almost a desperate plan, but the situation was desperate and nothing but boldness would serve. A frontal attack down the line of the trunk road might succeed but it would be at a terrible cost in lives, and a force less than fifteen hundred strong, with half of its task yet to do, and faced with an enemy of over five thousand, could not afford to risk a single life unnecessarily. There was cover on his right flank, where the woods were thick though not continuous, since there were gaps in them across which the troops would have to move and where they might be seen. It was a risk which he had to take and he would take it the more readily because of his knowledge of the mentality of his enemy. If the Sepoys were to see his movement, they could, with their enormous strength in cavalry and horse-drawn guns, take the initiative and fall on him while he was still moving towards a flank and the result might well be disastrous.

He had prepared a distraction for the enemy to occupy them in front, while his infantry were moving and, as at the Pandu Nuddhi, the volunteer cavalry were to provide it. There were only eighteen of them but, now that he had given them the Irregulars' horses, they were well mounted and, as soldiers, they were among the best men that he had. Nearly all of them were officers who had been left without employment when their regiments mutinied, so that they were used to responsibility and to acting on their own initiative. Captain Barrow, who commanded them, was the only real cavalryman among them and had already proved his ability to handle them on an occasion which needed not only courage but a spice of showmanship.

The eighteen horsemen trotted down the road, trying gallantly to look and sound like eight hundred and Barrow handled them cunningly, appearing and disappearing, darting from cover to cover, retracing his steps and emerging from somewhere in the rear, until it looked as if he had twenty troops and not one weak section at his disposal. The main body of the brigade began their move to the right flank behind the cover of the trees. A screen of skirmishers from the Madras Fusiliers preceded them and the Highlanders formed the vanguard. The guns came next, followed by the 64th and the 84th, and the Sikhs were in the rear.

For a time the enemy were deluded by the impudent assurance of Barrow's horsemen and, one after another, their guns opened fire with ranging shots on the road. Havelock rode with the main body, alert for any sign that the enemy had detected his movement. They crossed one gap in the trees and another, but, at a third, their red coats must have shown up against the drab colour of the scrub and the green of the trees and the enemy saw them.

They were racing against time now and the odds were against them.

The ground was sodden and the miserable oxen in the gun-teams strained and slipped as the wheels sank into the mud. One gun was bogged down, and the native drivers plied their goads mercilessly, while British gunners and infantry flung their weight behind the gun-carriage and threw down stones and branches under the wheels. They were all but clear of the woods when the first ranging shots came over, falling short of them.

As they broke clear of cover and began their wheel to the left, more guns got the range and men began to fall. The Fusiliers worked their way forward, bringing the long-range fire of the Enfields to bear, and, behind that thin screen, the regiments fell into their alignment with the steadiness of a parade. Maude and his gunners, by tremendous efforts, managed to bring a few guns into action but their range was too short and they had to move forward again. Havelock realised that for the moment he could count on little support from his artillery, desperately though the men worked the guns. The Nana Sahib had thoroughly looted the magazine at Cawnpore and had found in it guns of a far heavier calibre and longer range than any which Havelock could bring against him. Under the weight of that fire the British line steadily formed into echelon with the 78th Highlanders leading on the right, and Havelock gave the word for the attack.

As the infantry moved forward they could see the uniformed figures behind the village walls and in the groves of mango trees and they heard the taunting sound of the Sepoy bands. They were playing a popular tune of the moment, 'Cheer, boys, Cheer'. The Highlanders, in the lead, ignored the advice, marching on in grim silence until they were within seventy yards of the front line of the enemy. Then their pipes suddenly screamed defiance, and they fired one volley and went in with the bayonet, the 64th coming up on their left and a little behind them. They stormed the first defences, though the enemy, being behind walls and breastworks, fought more stubbornly than usual. Slowly the 78th drove them back to their second line, a position in a little village a few hundred yards in rear.

The British were almost astride of the cantonment road now and the Highlanders swept on, leaving it on their left, while the 64th and the 84th with the Sikhs crossed over and assaulted a position on the far side of it, between the trunk and cantonment roads. Havelock was up with the front line and once his gay question, 'Now, lads, who's going to take the village first, the 64th or the Highlanders?' brought from the 78th the storm of cheering which they had denied to his more formal address. As he had said, they would cheer soon enough when they saw the enemy in front of them.

It was at this stage of the battle that Havelock, as he said later in his report, 'decided to risk a charge of my cavalry'. Barrow's eighteen had advanced up the trunk road without loss and he launched them into the mass of retreating Sepoys, though the native cavalry had by now moved gingerly up to their support.

By the side of the trunk road the Army of Cawnpore rested for a brief spell to watch a miracle. Barrow and his horsemen came on at the gallop and the Sepoys broke and ran before them. The native cavalry thought better of their rash gesture and rode off. Four of the British horsemen fell in the charge, but the rest came out of the mêlée, sweating, covered with blood, triumphant. The infantry sent up a tremendous cheer, and the pipes shrilled in salute, as Havelock cantered up to the cavalry, crying out, 'Well done the Cavalry! I am proud to command you.'

For a short time there was a lull in the fight. The enemy had retired to their last defensive position, where they had their heaviest gun, a 24-pounder. The British were completely exhausted. They had marched and fought all the previous day and their night's rest had been short and troubled by the rain. Above all, they had hardly eaten for over twenty-four hours. At the end of the day before, they had flung themselves down where they stood, longing only for sleep, too tired to cook the meat which had been sent up. The only meat available for the army on that march was beef, freshly killed by the regimental butchers, who marched in rear of the column with their herd of skinny, ancient cattle. In that hot, steamy atmosphere, the meat had turned bad in the night, so that even the famished men threw it away with loathing and faced their duty with bellies empty except for a few hard biscuits and the generous issue of porter. What little effect the liquor had had on them had passed with the morning's work and their strength was all but gone.

The enemy, based on Cawnpore and its surrounding countryside, lacked nothing but courage, and now, seeing the British, as they thought, fought to a standstill, they gathered their energies for the counter-attack. Even the Nana Sahib ventured near to the firing line in the hope of animating his followers, or, as his many enemies said, borne there, all unwilling, by his escort. The cavalry moved up nearer in rear and some of the more venturous began to advance on the flanks.

Havelock, who was up in the front line of the British, saw that the real crisis of the fight had been reached. So far his men had done all that could be asked of mortal men, but now they must do more. Their advance had left the guns far behind and there was no hope of enough delay to get them up. The last and supreme effort must be made by the infantry, and they had barely strength to stand. He knew that the Highlanders at least would find it where no strength was and he rode along the line and called to them. They answered the call of the pipes, as they had never failed to answer since the days of Bruce, and the line reformed and made ready to go forward. Havelock, looking along it, suddenly saw that the 64th were not moving, but were still lying on the ground, but even as he looked, a mounted figure appeared at full gallop going in their direction and pulled up before them. Before his father's eyes Henry Havelock turned his horse as the men rose to follow him and rode before them straight for the muzzle of the big gun. Young Henry, as A.D.C. to his father, should have been beside him, but since Beatson, the D.A.A.Q., was all but dead of cholera, he had been employed on a multitude of duties in different parts of the field. Beatson, ill as he was and unable to sit on his horse, had had himself taken to the field in a rough cart and had gone forward with the cavalry in it, cheering them on till his strength failed and he sank back, a dying man. Henry had taken over part of his duties and now, seeing the 64th, as he thought, unable or unwilling to go forward, he had ridden across to lead them into action.

The incident so filled Havelock with pardonable pride that it betrayed him later into one of his rare errors of judgement, in recommending his son for the Victoria Cross. In the heat of action and at some distance from that part of the front, he was easily betrayed into thinking that Henry's bravery had roused the 64th who were hanging back, but the suggestion was afterwards bitterly resented by the regiment and especially by Major Stirling who was in command and was naturally furious at the idea that his men would not follow him but went at the bidding of a damned young pup of a staff officer. Maude, who deals at some length with the incident in his memoirs, gives what is probably the true explanation. The stupid convention of the day required the field officers of an infantry regiment to ride, not walk, before their men when going into action. Stirling, like so many of the other officers, had had to provide himself with whatever horse he could get from a rascally horse-dealer, and his mount was a pig-headed native pony with a mouth like iron. It had been so maddened by the firing that it had become almost unmanageable, and when Stirling remounted after the short break, it was so wild that he could do nothing with it. It was while he was dismounting and making ready to advance on foot that young Havelock, in his pardonable keenness and excitement, had seen the 64th hanging back and had called on them to follow him.

Whatever the reason for his action, no one could dispute his courage, and his father, watching anxiously, saw the explosion of the 24-pounder and heard its roar. Then the scene was shrouded in smoke, and when it cleared away, Henry, untouched, still sat his horse, and the 64th were pouring over the breastwork into the enemy's position. At the same moment the skirl of pipes and the fierce Highland shout heralded their assault, and the whole line went in with levelled bayonets and stormed the village. Under their attack the enemy broke and fled for their lives. The Nana Sahib was among the first to leave the field and to reach Cawnpore. He only paused there long enough for the characteristic action of ordering the murder of the last survivor of the British prisoners, a lady who had been pregnant when she was captured and had been saved at the entreaty of the Nana's harem. She and her new-born child were both shot by the Nana's command, and, with this parting gesture of spite, he mounted a fresh horse and rode out of Cawnpore in the direction of his house at Bithur.

As far as the British were concerned, he was never seen again, diligently though they sought him. There were many rumours of his direction and it was said that he had managed to make his escape northwards, and across the border into Nepal and thence to Tibet. It is thought that there he met his end, perhaps alone and starving on some hillside, pursued by a terror which would never let him rest; that he starved to death there in the mountains, while the vultures wheeled above him, waiting for their prey. It may be that, in his last distraught moments, he heard, in the wind and in the cry of the obscene birds, an echo of the sounds which had come from the lighted window of the slaughter-house at Cawnpore.

The Sepoy Army was broken and the way to Cawnpore lay open, but the British were spent. Once again they had nothing to eat and their Brigadier was glad to make his supper off a bottle of porter and a biscuit which he found in his son's haversack. They lay down and slept where they fell, in the mud and among the shattered trees, with the dead for company and the cries of the wounded for their night-song. They were too tired to feel triumphant, to feel anything but the animal craving for sleep: too tired even to wonder about the fate of the women and children in Cawnpore, still, for all they knew, held in the Nana's prison. There was no attempt at pursuit, since the cavalry could hardly raise a trot, and once again Havelock saw his triumph slip through his hands for lack of the means to follow it up. They were only two miles from Cawnpore, from which, all night long, a stream of fugitives poured out and took any road of escape which might lead them away from the reckoning to come. Such townspeople as could not leave were hastily collecting bunches of fruit and vegetables as propitiatory offerings against the next day. By midnight there was not a Sepoy in the town and as many of the population as could contrive it had gone after them. The rest waited in fear behind closed doors. No light showed in the streets and there was silence over the cantonments, over the shattered entrenchment where Wheeler's heroic party had fought and died, and over the courtyard where the bodies of the murdered lay in the well.

CHAPTER XIX

PREPARATION FOR THE RELIEF OF LUCKNOW (1857)

'SOLDIERS! YOUR General is satisfied and more than satisfied.' Havelock's Order of the Day, published after the battle of Cawnpore had the authentic ring of the First Empire:

> 'He has never seen steadier or more devoted troops; but your labours are only beginning. Between the 7th and the 16th, you have, under the Indian sun of July, marched 126 miles and fought four actions. But your comrades at Lucknow are in peril; Agra is besieged; Delhi is still the focus of mutiny and rebellion. You must make great sacrifices if you are to obtain great results. Three cities have to be saved; two strong places to be dis-blockaded. Your General is confident that he can effect all these things and restore this part of India to tranquillity, if you will only second him with your efforts, and if your discipline is equal to your valour.'

The words had the sound of rolling gun-wheels and clattering cuirassiers, but the army of Cawnpore, when it crawled into the town next day, looked more like the end of the Moscow retreat. The men were weary, hungry, and clad in an assortment of dirty rags. Above all they were utterly dispirited. Before day broke a reconnaissance party of the cavalry had ridden into the city and found it bare of troops. They had brought back with them the news of the massacre of the women and children, and it had taken all the heart out of the soldiers, who felt angrily that they had endured so much for no result. The story was too circumstantial to be doubted and it left them with a burning desire to plunder and kill and destroy. Their Brigadier's words about their discipline may sound cold and ungrateful after all that they had achieved, but he knew them only too well and he knew what to expect when they should be turned loose in the town.

The soldiers were not only tired and hungry but thirsty too and there was liquor in the cellars of Cawnpore. He could hold them for a few hours but, as soon as they were dismissed from duty, they would become a pack of ravening wolves, and by daylight half of them would be sodden wrecks and some of them dead. There would be blazing roofs and corpses lying in the gutters, women screaming for help and all the bestiality that always followed when a British force went to pieces. He was told, as he entered the town, of the death of Henry Lawrence at Lucknow on the 4th of July. Lucknow was his next objective, but, now that Lawrence's strong hand and stout heart were gone, he dared not think of what might happen there. He and Lawrence had been friends for sixteen years, and, though their various duties kept them for the most part in different districts of India, so that they met but seldom, they had formed a high and mutual regard. Havelock had written his last letter to Lawrence on the eve of leaving Allahabad, saying:

> 'I march towards Cawnpore tomorrow with a thousand Europeans and six guns and, if safely united to Renaud's force, shall muster about 1500 Europeans and eight guns. With these I am ready to fight a battle to relieve Cawnpore and, holding that place with a detachment, to march to your aid.'

He had marched to Cawnpore and arrived too late to relieve it and now he learned that Lawrence was beyond human aid. He had achieved the all but impossible and he rode into Cawnpore with his enemies scattered before him, surely as sadly as ever victorious general rode into conquered city. He rode alone, a little in front of his staff, with his chin sunk on his breast while his exhausted Arab charger stumbled and slipped in the mud of the track.

Sherer, the civilian magistrate, who followed later in the rear, has described that entry. As he rode in, with one other companion, he was met by a man with a small kettle-drum, who strutted before them, plying his sticks and loudly proclaiming the restoration of British rule. (Sherer was shrewd enough to reflect that probably a few hours earlier the drum had sounded for the Nana Sahib.)

> 'We passed through some streets [he goes on] till we reached the principal thoroughfare—the Chouk—at the head of which stood the Kotwali, a two-storied building, with arches in front, forming a balcony above. Here we dismounted, ascended the upper story, and were almost immediately surrounded by a crowd of people, many of them Bengalees. They professed themselves delighted with our return: but were rather afraid of the soldiers, and thought that, if measures of retaliation were taken, the innocent might be confounded with the guilty.'

They were very loyal in Cawnpore that day. Sherer remarked that the Bengali is always ready to write and one of them had set up a table and was busily turning out placards which he proffered for signature. Soon many houses bore the proud announcement, 'This house belongs to one Mokerjee, very loyal subject. Please not to molest.' But there were traces of less friendly sentiments here and there on the walls, from which the natives had not had time to remove the big posters with which the Nana had tried to raise the failing courage of his adherents.

Havelock led the brigade on to the cavalry parade ground and they were given temporary quarters in the barracks and stables. So far they had been under discipline and no harm had come to the town. The natives crowded round them with offerings of fruit and flowers and, which was much more to their taste, with tales of rich stores of wine and spirits, all to be had for the taking. The soldiers listened eagerly and, as soon as they had been dismissed from parade, hurried into the streets of the town.

There was no rest for their Brigadier, who went off at once to make a tour of the hospitals—poor makeshift places which were short of every kind of medical necessity. They would soon lack even the wretched palliasses and heaps of straw which had to serve for beds for dysentery had attacked the brigade and, within the last few days, cholera too had appeared. In all their fights they had not lost above fifty men killed, but between four and five hundred had fallen by sunstroke or disease.

As usual, Havelock found time to write to his wife, and also to his brother-in-law, Marshman, pouring out the pride which he felt in Harry's courage and in his own victory, but which he could only express to those who knew and loved him. He wrote to his wife:

> 'I never saw so brave a youth as the boy Harry. He placed himself opposite to the muzzle of a gun that was scattering death into the 64th Queen's and led on the regiment under a shower of grape to its capture. This finished the fight. The grape was deadly but he calm as if telling George stories about India. Lawrence has died of his wounds . . . at Lucknow. I am marching to relieve it. Trust in God and pray for us. All India is up in arms against us, and everywhere round me things are looking black. Thank God for His special mercies to me.'

Only to Hannah could he show the discouragement and doubt which beset him now that the strain was for a moment relaxed. To Marshman he wrote more cheerfully:

> 'I bivouacked in good spirits, though without dinner, my waterproof coat serving me for a couch on the damp ground. So you see I am become my trumpeter in my old age.'

If he blew his trumpet loudly it was to keep up his own spirits, and when darkness fell he could keep melancholy at bay no longer. He dined in his quarters with his son for company, and later the boy told how his father sat silent at the table, hardly touching his food but resting his head on his hand. After an unusually long silence, Harry heard him say to himself, in a voice so low that he could hardly catch the words, 'If the worst comes to the worst, we can but die with our swords in our hands.'

In the town of Cawnpore there was noise and tumult as the troops fell on the liquor and, forgetting all that their officers had told them, broke into houses to steal and destroy. Many of them had been to look at the entrenchment where Wheeler and his heroic party had held out so long and had marvelled at the tale of their endurance behind that flimsy defence. Some of them went further and penetrated into the courtyard of the Bibighur, the building where the women had been slaughtered. The house stood as the murderers had left it, not yet cleansed of the hideous traces of their work. The men saw the marks of sabre cuts on wall and pillar, noting that many were low down as though the blows had been struck at victims who knelt in supplication or from weakness. They saw the marks of the bullets on the walls where the Sepoys had fired high, to miss the women, and the splashes of blood on the walls. A few spoke of seeing torn and slashed clothing and small shoes and garments which had been worn by children. One or two, bolder or more avid than the rest, peered over the edge of the well and saw in the failing light a tangle of naked limbs.

The marvel is that worse things were not done in the town that night, when the men poured out of the Bibigurgh with their weapons in their hands, burning to kill the first natives whom they saw. There was looting and destruction, but the wine shops and the cellars took their toll of the famished, exhausted men before they could glut their anger, and dysentery and cholera took over the work which the wine shops had begun. By morning the army of Cawnpore were a dishevelled rabble, falling in the streets to die where they lay, besieging the hospitals for help, ignoring the efforts of their officers to bring them back to sanity. They had forgotten all thought of Lucknow where their comrades waited, relying on them, all sense of their duty and of their regiments. They had only one thought, to drink and burn and kill and drink again in the hope that they might forget what they had seen in the house and in the well.

It was not the least achievement of Havelock's career that he brought that frenzied mob back to their duty. He had acted swiftly, knowing what their reaction would be, and knowing that nothing but the utmost severity would have any effect.

Before he rested that night he had formed a Provost party and appointed a subaltern of the Madras Fusiliers as Provost-Major, giving him summary powers to check the disorder. Out of such men as still retained a sense of their duty he placed sentries over all the wine stores, ordering them to shoot without argument any man, white or black, who tried to enter. As soon as the guards were posted, he sent the Commissariat men to buy up and hold every drop of liquor on which they could lay their hands. In his report to Sir Patrick Grant he explained, 'It will thus be guarded by a few men. If it remained in Cawnpore, it would require half my force to keep it from being drunk up by the other half, and I should scarcely have a sober soldier in camp.' The Sikhs, always the most accomplished of plunderers, were foremost in the work, and deeply resented the loss of an opportunity to seize the drink and sell it to the Europeans at a colossal profit. Plainly Havelock Sahib was as officious and as callous as had been Neill Sahib at Allahabad. Both European and native soldier knew that Havelock Sahib meant what he said in the proclamation which he issued to the troops.

> 'The marauding in this camp exceeds the disorders which supervened on the short-lived triumph of the miscreant Nana Sahib. A Provost-Marshal has been appointed with special powers and instructions to hang up in their uniform all British soldiers that plunder. This shall not be an idle threat. Commanding officers have received the most distinct warnings on the subject.'

The soldiers cursed him but they obeyed when they saw the gallows which the Provost men were erecting in the streets and found that they carried cats-o'-nine-tails with which they lustily administered not less than two dozen strokes to any man who could not show a pass allowing him to go out of camp. But Havelock was wise as well as severe, and, as a Christian, he knew the meaning of the prayer, 'Lead us not into temptation'. He had determined to move his men to a place where they would be less subject to the temptations of the town, and he had selected the north-western point of the cantonments near the Grand Trunk Road. His action was criticised at the time on the grounds that it was not strategically an ideal position, as though, with that hell of trouble on his hands, he could find the time for reconnaissance and a nice appreciation of the military situation. His one thought was to get what remained of his brigade away from the streets, the brothels and the cellars, into a place where he could restore them to a sense of their duty and of the urgency of the situation. Even so—as most critics afterwards admitted—in choosing the position near Newab-Gunj, he had kept in mind at least one possible danger from without. The Gwalior troops had mutinied and his information was that they were advancing towards Cawnpore. If that were so, the shortest and easiest way for them would be the Trunk Road and he had chosen a place where his guns could command it. There, with drill and discipline, he set to work to restore his brigade to the fighting force which they had been, and again he realised that distraction would do more than severity.

There had been no definite information as to the whereabouts of the Nana Sahib, since he had left Cawnpore, but rumour said that he had gone to his palace in Bithur, and Havelock decided to test the truth of it and to smoke him out. He selected for the task the Madras Fusiliers, who, with their memories of the relentless discipline of Neill, their late Commanding Officer, were less out of hand than any of the other troops. The Fusiliers were glad of the chance to see the palace, of whose splendour and wealth the wildest rumours were in circulation, but they arrived to find it deserted, and they were deeply disappointed not to find the famous gold plate, which had been hidden or carried off. There was plenty of plunder to be had, in spite of the absence of the main attraction, and the Fusiliers seized all that they could carry and burned the palace to the ground.

All this time Havelock had never lost sight of the urgency of his mission to relieve Lucknow and he was determined to start before the end of the month. Sickness had so much reduced his force that his urgent need was for troops and he telegraphed to Sir Patrick Grant again and again pressing his request. At the same time he ordered Neill to leave Allahabad and march to reinforce him with every man he could muster. Neill, for his part, was equally anxious, for he had hanged every native within miles of the town and was beginning to lack occupation. During the course of his most improper correspondence with Grant he had received a letter into which he read a good deal more than Grant had probably intended. Grant, too, was urging him to march for Cawnpore, while he expressed the utmost admiration for the achievements of Havelock and his brigade, adding:

> 'But his health is not strong, and the season is very trying; it is urgently necessary, therefore, that provision should be made for placing the command of the column in tried hands of known and assured efficiency, in whom perfect confidence can be placed, in case Havelock should become from any cause unfit for duty. You have been selected for the post and accordingly you will proceed with every practicable expedition to join Havelock, making over the command of Allahabad to the next senior officer.'

To a mind such as Neill's this was practically an invitation to succeed Havelock, whose seniority and continued good health were a source of grievance. He pressed on as fast as he could towards Cawnpore, leaving behind him a long list of instructions for his successor, since he could never believe in the efficiency of anyone except himself. He had already sent forward such reinforcements as had reached him and brought another small party with him.

He arrived in Cawnpore on 20th July to find a somewhat bleak reception awaiting him. Neill probably imagined that his correspondence with Grant remained a profound secret between the two of them, forgetting that Havelock was in communication with Headquarters and that, with his long experience and wide acquaintance on the staff, he was likely to get to hear of most things which were going on.

In his diary, Neill recorded, 'I was well received by General Havelock'. His standards of cordiality must have been low, or his reluctance to set down the true facts strong. Most men would have considered the reception anything but favourable, for Havelock greeted him at once with the ominous words, 'Now, General Neill, we had better understand each other; you have no power or authority while I am here, and you are not to issue a single order.' Neill had just been promoted to Brigadier-General, but Havelock was in command and had no intention of sharing his authority. He knew Neill's efficiency and valued it, and it was his intention to leave him in command at Cawnpore, while he marched to Lucknow.

Neill's intentions had probably been exactly the opposite, especially after reading Grant's letter. His ill-nature found an outlet in a series of letters to various friends in the army, in which he complained of everything which Havelock had done or had failed to do since he had arrived at Cawnpore. The encampment, he wrote, was the most unsuitable that could have been chosen, the troops were out of hand and there appeared to be no compliance with orders. Commanding officers made no attempt to control their men.

The chief obstacle in the way of an immediate advance on Lucknow, apart from the permanent one of lack of men, was the problem of crossing the River Ganges which ran north of the town. The recent rains had swollen it to a breadth of over sixteen hundred yards and the mutineers, in their flight, had destroyed the bridge of boats which had spanned it. Havelock, as soon as he had entered Cawnpore, had reconnoitred the position and had set to work to restore the bridge. He soon met with almost insuperable difficulties. He had no pontoon equipment and no hope of getting any, so that he had to rely on boats for his bridge. But nearly all the boats had been destroyed or carried off and it was almost impossible, in that unfriendly country, to persuade boatmen to sell or hire their craft or to take any part in the work. He had learned that the mutineers were in strength on the far side of the river, and were so near that they could resist his attempt to cross, since the passage of the river by a brigade with guns must inevitably take several days.

In his telegram of 28th July, he warned Grant of the difficulties which he faced and of the further danger which he must face, should he, after relieving Lucknow, want to return to Cawnpore.

> 'In reply to your Excellency's telegram of the 26th, I beg to state that I should consider it certain that I must incur the risk of serious loss in an attempt to recross the Ganges to Cawnpore, even if I had been reinforced by the remnant of the garrison at Lucknow. The chances of relieving that place are at the same time hourly multiplying against us. . . . The communications and much information, orally derived from spies, convince me of the extreme delicacy and difficulty of any operation to relieve Colonel Inglis. . . . It shall be attempted however at any risk and the result faithfully reported.'

He ends with a repetition of his request for more men:

> 'My whole force amounts to 1500 men of whom 1200 are British, and ten guns, imperfectly equipped and manned.'

The letter is characteristic of Havelock, in that he neither minimises the difficulties of the undertaking, nor allows them to turn him from his task. He had to provide a garrison for Cawnpore, and for the holding of his crossing-place over the Ganges after he had marched, and he knew now that the Gwalior mutineers were only about forty-five miles off and were some 3,000 strong. He could spare Neill no more than 300 men for the garrison, which Neill considered inadequate, as indeed it was. But Neill's superior officer proposed to march, with an impassable river in his rear and a force of unknown strength somewhere within a day's march of his route, taking with him fewer than 1,500 men. It was a fearful risk for both of them. Havelock knew it and decided to take it, and he was not to be dissuaded by Neill's reluctance to shoulder his own share.

Crommelin, the Chief Engineer, and Colonel Fraser-Tytler had accomplished wonders in the collection of boats for the bridge and of material and labour for the fortification of a bridgehead on the bank. Cawnpore had yielded several hundreds of unwilling workers, who were reinforced by volunteers from the brigade, and at last a use was found for the Irregular Cavalry who had behaved so badly at Fatehpur. Their horses and arms had been taken away from them, and now they were furnished with shovels and set to dig. Tytler supervised the work with the help of Captain Havelock, who had taken over the duties of D.A.A.Q.M.G. on Beatson's death, and at last they were ready for a start. Considering that the brigade had entered Cawnpore on 17th July, had suffered heavily from sickness, and had had to collect all their material and labour for the bridge-building, it was little less than a miracle that in eight days they should be ready to attempt the next stage of their task. On the 25th Havelock sat on his horse by the side of the Ganges and watched the first details of the brigade begin their crossing, and, during the next three days, the rest of the brigade went over and all the stores and transport which they had been able to collect were put across.

On the 29th the brigade began their march for Lucknow. They had been reinforced with infantry and a very few gunners, but they had no cavalry to screen their movement and to reconnoitre in front of them till Havelock overcame the difficulty by selecting about forty infantrymen who had some knowledge of horses, mounting them, and telling them that they were cavalry.

He has been much criticised for venturing with so little prospect of success, and there were not wanting detractors who said that his recent victories had gone to his head and inflated his ideas of his ability. His own correspondence with Grant gives the lie to the suggestion. He went, in full awareness of the terrible risk which he was incurring, because Lucknow had to be relieved and there was no one else to do it. It was not perhaps a safe move, but the British power in India had not been won and was not held by safe men, but by men who, after counting the cost, decided to attempt—and often achieved—the seemingly impossible.

CHAPTER XX

'THE OLD GENTLEMAN' (1857)

AS SOON as Havelock had marched out of Cawnpore, Neill took over command of the town and turned his attention to the task of avenging the murders. On the day when he took command he issued his order, dated 27th July, which was soon to be notorious. He himself wrote of it to a friend;

> 'I issued the following order, which, however objectionable to some of our Brahminised elderly gentlemen, I think suited to the occasion.'
>
> [After directing the filling in of the well by a British party under an officer, the order goes on:]
>
> '"The house in which they were butchered and which is stained with their blood, will not be cleaned or washed by their countrymen. But Brigadier Neill has determined that every stain of that innocent blood shall be cleared up and wiped out, previous to their execution, by such of the miscreants as may be hereafter apprehended, who took active part in the mutiny, to be selected according to their rank, caste and degree of guilt. Each miscreant, after sentence of death is pronounced upon him, will be taken down to the house in question, under a guard and will be forced into cleaning a small portion of the blood-stains. The task will be made as revolting to his feelings as possible, and the Provost-Marshal will use the lash in forcing anyone objecting to complete his task. After properly cleaning up his portion, the culprit is to be hanged and for this purpose a gallows is to be erected close to hand."'

It is difficult not to feel repulsion at such detailed cruelty, though it may fairly be said that the murderers of Cawnpore deserved no mercy. No one who has not seen such a sight as that house of butchery must have presented is in a position to judge the actions of those who entered it a few hours after the horror had been done. There are more revolting details of the way in which the punishment was carried out, the object of which was to defile a man's caste before his death so that he might hope for no mercy beyond the grave—of Brahmins, who were flogged into acting as sweepers, the greatest defilement possible for them, and of lower castes, who were not given brooms but were made to lick up the blood with their tongues. It may well be that Neill was thinking of Havelock when he wrote of 'Brahminised elderly gentlemen', for Havelock, who believed in the utmost severity allowed by martial law, did not believe in cruelty. Several times during those days he was heard to say, 'After all, we do not want to be like them'.

Neill had no compunction and the order is important as revealing his state of mind only a few days before his open insolence to Havelock. Undoubtedly power had gone to his head, and he resented the fact that Havelock was still his superior. An artillery officer, who was much in his company at Cawnpore, has written that Neill used openly to speak disrespectfully of Havelock, careless of who might be listening. He had, for instance, the habit of referring to him as 'the Old Gentleman' and said that 'the Old Gentleman looks on me as an heir-at-law prospective and there is no wonder that he dislikes me'.

Neill's own diary is even more illuminating. He records his doings in Cawnpore, just before Havelock left, in such a way as to lead the reader to imagine that he was the directing mind and that Havelock ran after him like a lackey and waited for his orders. Few people who knew Havelock would think such a story likely.

In justice to Neill, it must be admitted that his situation at Cawnpore was precarious enough to try the nerves of the strongest men. His total force, apart from invalids and convalescents, amounted to 300 men, and the Gwalior contingent, ten times as strong, might be upon him any time. He could expect no help from Havelock who was deeply committed on the far side of the Ganges, and, though reinforcements were on the way from Allahabad, it must be a matter of some time before they could reach him in any strength.

Before many days had passed both he and Havelock realised that it might be a very long time indeed before these reinforcements would be available, owing to a serious outbreak at Dinapore. On the day on which Havelock crossed the Ganges, 3,000 native troops, who were stationed there and had so far been loyal, broke into mutiny. There were two British units on the station, the 10th Foot and a wing of the 37th Foot, but, though they turned out against the mutineers, their efforts were nullified by the divisional general, Lloyd. He had done well in an unimportant mutiny earlier at Santal, but he was one of those officers who persisted beyond all reason in trusting his Sepoys, and his supineness allowed the mutinous regiments to escape from the station without fighting and without pursuit, though pursuit would have done little good, since there were no cavalry available. The most serious result of this outbreak was that, as Dinapore was on the route from Calcutta to Cawnpore, the forces threatening the line of communications were suddenly increased by 3,000 well-trained and well-armed men.

Grant, who was just about to hand over command to Campbell, decided that the 10th and 37th must first be employed to clear this danger away from the route and also stopped the advance of the main bodies of the 5th Fusiliers and the 90th Rifles who were on the way to Dinapore. There can be no criticism of Grant's action. Havelock was now operating at the end of a line of communications stretching back over 900 miles to Calcutta and it would be useless to reinforce him until this line had been made safe, as along it all his supplies of men, food and ammunition must come. But it made the position of Neill at Cawnpore and Havelock beyond the Ganges desperate in the extreme. At the most modest estimate, their total strength of less than 2,000, not all of whom were fit for action, was surrounded by some 10,000 of the enemy.

It is almost certain that if the mutiny at Dinapore had broken out only a few days earlier, the news would have reached Havelock in time for him to stop his advance on Lucknow. Nor—though he did not know it at the time—would it have mattered very much if he had been delayed, for there had been an inexplicable mistake made at Lucknow about the amount of food which was held in store. Colonel McLeod Innes, who was in Lucknow and wrote the story of the siege, says that the miscalculation was such that the garrison actually believed that they had only one eighth of the food which was in store in various buildings. The mistake was not discovered until the force commanded by Havelock and Outram entered the Residency on 26th September. The margin of error seems almost too great to be believed, but Innes was in a position to know, and that it is not far of the mark is proved by the fact that, though Havelock's relieving force brought no food with them, and though the siege continued for seven weeks after their arrival, since the combined forces were not strong enough to break out, even so there was enough food in the stores to supply the increased garrison and all the civilians until the arrival of Campbell in November.

Henry Lawrence had taken every possible precaution for the provision of the Residency position when he first decided to occupy it in May. He had laid in enormous quantities of grain, ammunition and every sort of food which could be stored without loss, and he had also collected within the defences a large herd of cattle for meat. There was an unfailing water supply and altogether the city was well able to face a siege of several months without going short or even on to half-rations. By mischance no proper system of accounting for the provisions and no record of what was stored were compiled. The siege began on 30th June immediately after a small and unsuccessful affair at Chinhut, when Lawrence had attempted to defeat a body of mutineers and had himself been routed. In the battle, the chief officer of the Commissariat was wounded and put out of action for some time and so was unable to give attention to the disposition and checking of the stores. When Sir Henry Lawrence died a few days later, there seems to have been nobody in Lucknow with the least idea as to what food they had and where it was kept. On Lawrence's death, authority in the Residency was divided between Major Banks, the civilian, and Colonel Inglis, the commandant of the garrison, until Banks was killed and Inglis assumed command over both military and civilians.

The result of this chain of mishaps was that Inglis was totally misinformed about the supply position and, in consequence, about the time for which his garrison could expect to hold out. In trying to let Havelock know the position, he naturally gave him an entirely wrong impression of the urgency of it, giving him to understand that by 10th September, even on reduced rations, as they then were, the garrison and their families would be actually starving.

At the beginning of the siege there were in the Residency and in a secondary position, called the Mutcjhi Bawn, a total of 3,000 people, of whom 1,720 were combatants. Of the rest, there were over five hundred women and children and over six hundred natives. The investing force never fell below 20,000. So close was the investment that it was almost impossible for the garrison to communicate with the outside world. One or two devoted native runners succeeded in passing through the cordon on perhaps half a dozen occasions, and it was one of these who gave Havelock 10th September as the day when existence would become impossible for the garrison. It was perhaps fortunate that a later and more desperate message from Inglis which implied that starvation was very near never reached Havelock, and that the same fate befell a message which he sent reporting his inability to get through without more troops and his intention to return to Cawnpore to await them. The receipt of either could only have increased alarm and despondency in the recipient.

Though no word of the intention had yet reached the brigade, the

Governor-General had decided to replace Havelock by Sir James Outram, who had just landed in India after handing over the remains of his command in Persia. It was a monstrous piece of injustice and one which it is difficult to understand, unless it were that, as Grant had suggested, the authorities at Calcutta were really afraid that Havelock's age and state of health might at any time betray him and make him incapable of command, perhaps at an awkward moment. Outram was much younger and a major-general and, as he was without employment, there was something, from the strictly military standpoint, to be said for the appointment, but from any standpoint of justice or gratitude it was abominable. Outram himself was disturbed when he first learned of the intention, which he did while on board and returning from Persia. At first he was minded to refuse it, and said to Colonel Napier, his Chief-of-Staff, that, if he went at all, it would be in his civil capacity, though he soon found that such an arrangement would be unworkable, and adopted a hardly less unhappy compromise. Obviously he thought that Havelock was being shabbily treated and deeply regretted that he must be an assenting party.

On 29th September, when Havelock began his advance, he must have thought that he was leading an even more hopeless venture than in fact he was. His position was desperate enough in all truth. Cawnpore, his only advanced base, was held by 300 men against possible attack by 3,000—and the 300 were commanded by an officer of whom he was beginning to have grave suspicions. In front of him were probably another 3,000 and beyond them an investing army of 20,000, most of whom could easily be detached to meet his advance. Behind him lay a threatened line of communications over 900 miles long. In front of him a garrison to be relieved before starvation compelled them to surrender. Behind him, too, was the memory of the murders at Cawnpore. There were women and children in Lucknow who would inevitably meet the same fate unless he could save them.

It is little to be wondered at that the officers and men who marched with him found him more exacting, more outspoken in his criticism, more intolerant of failure. He was in good health, but he was an ageing man and he had made heavy demands on his small reserves of physical strength. He was haunted by a sense of failure and a feeling that if he had only reached Cawnpore two or three days earlier he might have averted the final tragedy. It was not a wholly rational feeling, for his earlier arrival would only probably have precipitated the murders and not prevented them, but a man in his position, strained to the last point and carrying such a burden, has little opportunity or peace of mind for analysing and rationalising his fears. He became in those days a man with an obsession—to reach Lucknow before that should happen there which had happened at Cawnpore. Sickness had broken out again in the brigade as soon as they crossed the Ganges, and every day cholera and dysentery claimed new victims. The troops were exhausted in body and soul and more than once there was a perceptible trace of sullenness about them. They had done all that they had been asked to do, and more than most men could have done, and they were being asked to do even more. Havelock's men trusted and obeyed him, seeing how carelessly he exposed his own body to the enemy's fire, realising that his orders were always clear and unmistakable and that he was more careful of their lives than he was of his own. Many of his officers, and especially those nearest to him, marvelled at the agility of his brain and his resource on the battle-field. Officers and men alike felt the power of his drive, the remorseless thrust of his determination. Some of them guessed that he felt himself inspired by a higher power than his own, as his demands grew more imperative and his rebukes more scathing. But somehow an impression remains that the brigade felt that they were being driven rather than led. He made no concessions to weakness, to weariness or to sickness. Once, when a British battalion hesitated to attack an apparently impregnable position, he railed at them, promising that if they did not go at it, he would send others who would and put an everlasting shame on them. Once, after a fight in which they had given all that they had and yet failed to achieve all that he had set for them to do, he turned on them and told them that they had fought as if the cholera had seized their minds as well as their bodies.

The truth was that the brigade had reached the limit of their endurance. They could not understand—they could not be expected to understand—that Havelock had reached and passed beyond the end of his, any more than he could understand that the mysterious strength of spirit which held him up might be lacking to men not in the grip of his obsession.

When after eight days, in which he had fought four actions, he had to abandon his attempt and turn his back for a time on the enemy and on a Lucknow which he believed to be starving, it was the bitterest moment of a life which had not been lacking in them. It was the moment in which he learned that, after all that he had achieved, he was to be superseded; and it was, of all moments, the one which Neill chose for an open display of the insolence which he had cherished but had not dared to show before. From that moment, though he lived another nine or ten weeks, and though he was as skilful and as brave as ever, he was a spent force. His body bore him into Lucknow to die on a pallet bed in the Alum Bagh, but his spirit had died on that morning when he watched his troops re-cross the Ganges.

CHAPTER XXI

SUPERSEDED (1857)

WHILE THE brigade were crossing the Ganges on their outward march, Havelock's first care was to establish an advanced base a few miles beyond the river at Mungulwar. Here he could leave his stores and hither his sick and wounded could return. Should he have to fall back under pressure, here his rearguard could stand to cover the main body while they re-crossed. It was well that he did so, for he was to make constant use of it during the next fortnight, setting off from it three times and twice returning, victorious in battle but unable to press home his advantage, owing to sickness among his troops and lack of replacements. On 29th July they started with high hope. The brigade were restored to something like their old shape by the rest in Cawnpore and by Havelock's insistence on discipline. He was almost in a fever to advance from Mungulwar, the more so because the first miles of his march must lie through country where he would be tactically at a great disadvantage.

The road from Mungulwar lay for some miles on a raised causeway, on each side of which was marshy ground, which had been made almost impassable by the recent rains. If the enemy should catch him before he could reach more open ground he would have no room for manœuvre and would have to face them on a narrow front, which they could easily hold in depth, with their flanks protected by the marsh. At the far end of the causeway the ground rose, slightly but enough to give space for manœuvre to right and left of the road near to the town of Busherat-Gange. It was a name which his men were to know only too well before they had done with it, for each time that they advanced, the enemy stood to fight there.

On the 29th he had to fight before he had left the causeway. The enemy was alive to the advantage of meeting him before he had room to deploy and had sent forward a strong force with some twenty guns to occupy the village of Unao. There was nothing for it but to carry the position by a frontal attack and the brigade went at it with a rush, the Madras Fusiliers and the Highlanders leading.

The enemy fought stoutly in a protected position and under the cover of their guns, while Havelock could not bring his own artillery into action. He found that the opposition on this side of the Ganges was much more determined than anything which he had yet met. The Oudh regiments who had mutinied were among the best in the old Native Army, and the Oudh artillery in particular had earned a great reputation, which they did not disgrace, though they had disgraced themselves in every other way. There was fierce hand-to-hand fighting when the leading British troops had forced the first line and found themselves among the guns. The Oudh gunners fought valiantly for the protection of their guns and there were bitter struggles with rifle and bayonet in the houses of the village. But the British, now that they were refreshed and while they still burned with the memory of the sights of Cawnpore, were irresistible, and the mutineers withdrew leaving fifteen of their cherished guns behind them. Havelock would have been glad to have them, but he had no horses or cattle to carry them off, since what cattle he had barely sufficed to drag Maude's battery. He ordered the destruction of the captured guns and gave the order to advance again. His spies had told him that a fresh force of some 6,000 was advancing from the direction of Lucknow, and he knew that he must reach the end of the causeway if he were to meet it with any hope of success. It was a race for the first piece of open ground and the British won. They met the reinforced enemy at the town of Busherat-Gange.

Here there was dry ground on each flank and Havelock had room for his favourite turning movement. The Sepoys, as usual, took position in the cover of the walls and gardens and he sent the 78th at them, supported by the artillery, since here the ground was dry enough for Maude to bring his guns into action. The 64th were sent round by the right flank to strike the road again beyond the town and, if all went well, he had hopes of encircling the enemy and destroying them from front and rear. But, hard though the 64th tried, they could not quite make their encircling move before the enemy saw their danger and began to pull out. Havelock was in a fury when he saw his chance fading and the 64th felt the lash of his tongue, but they had reached the rear of the town too late to do anything but cut off a few stragglers.

The enemy had lost more than 400 in the fighting in the town and the British casualties amounted only to 88 in killed and wounded.

But 400 out of 6,000 compared favourably with 88 out of barely 1,500 and that was not the end of the British losses, which were more than doubled by sunstroke and sickness. The cholera marched with them and men fell, untouched by steel or bullet, and died by the roadside or among the captured guns.

They had advanced altogether 15 miles and had beaten the enemy twice, but they had lost a dangerous proportion of their tiny numbers and, after Busherat-Gange, they had fired away a third of their ammunition. There was nothing for it but to retire on to their base at Mungulwar, there to leave their sick and wounded, to replenish the ammunition reserves, and, if possible, to pick up some reinforcements. Havelock gave the order to retreat and on the morning of the 31st they reached Mungulwar. It was while he was there that the trouble between him and Neill came to a head. Neill had received reports of the fighting of the last two days and had passed them on to Headquarters with his own comments, which, it need hardly be said, were as adverse towards his superior as he could make them.

> 'As you know [he wrote to Calcutta], the first march brought him into contact with the enemy; he had one day's hard fighting on the 29th, beat him completely; we lost a number of men in the first affair, from some little mistake . . . but take the whole day's work, the loss was not much; nineteen guns were taken in all, but three, ordered to be brought up and secured by the Sikhs, were left behind, and taken away by the enemy; this left sixteen fine brass guns, most of them ours—one a brass 24 pounder. However all of these were destroyed by the General's order. The enemy were flying —the bridge they were so anxious about was ten or twelve miles off, our men in high spirits, blood up, etc., this was the time; but suddenly, on being ordered to fall in to march, instead of an advance it was a retreat.'

When Havelock returned to Mungulwar on 31st July he wrote to Neill, in Cawnpore, and asked for any reinforcements which he could send. If Neill had been a man of good heart or understanding, he would have known what a bitter disappointment Havelock was suffering, and if he had been a gentleman, he would have respected his feeling. Also, if he had been a soldier of any experience in command, he would have known that Havelock's statement that he needed 1,000 infantry and more guns to be a very modest one. If he had known the real meaning of discipline, he would not have written the letter with which he replied.

> 'My dear General,
>
> 'I late last night received yours of 5 p.m. yesterday. I deeply regret that you have fallen back one foot. The effect on our prestige is very bad in-

deed. Your camp was not pitched yesterday, before all manners of reports were rife in the city—that you had returned to get some guns, having lost all those which you took with you. In fact the belief among all is that you have been defeated and forced back. It has been most unfortunate your not bringing back any of the guns captured from the enemy. The natives will not believe that you have captured one. The effect of your retrograde movement will be very injurious to our cause everywhere and bring down upon us many who would otherwise have held off or even sided with us. . . . You talk of advancing as soon as reinforcements reach you. You require a battery and a thousand infantry. As regards the battery, half of Olphert's will be in this morning. The other half started yesterday or the day before from Allahabad. This will detain you five or six days more. As for the infantry you require, they are not to be had, and if you are to wait for them, Lucknow will follow the fate of Cawnpore. Agra will be invested. . . . You ought not to remain a day longer where you are. When the iron guns are sent to you, also the half-battery of artillery and the company of the 84th escorting, you ought to advance again and not halt until you have rescued, if possible, Lucknow. . . .'

The letter ends with the astonishing command, 'Return here sharp, for there is much to be done between this and Agra and Delhi.'

Havelock's answer to this piece of insolence must have penetrated even the armour of Neill's self-sufficiency. Neill himself described it as 'a terrific reply'. After describing Neill's letter as 'one of the most extraordinary which I have ever perused', Havelock wrote:

'I wrote to you confidentially on the state of affairs. You send me back a letter of censure on my measures, reproof and advice for the future. There must be an end to these proceedings at once. I do not want, and will not submit to receive any of them from an officer under my command, be his experience what it may. Understand this distinctly, and a consideration of the inconvenience which would arise to the public service at this moment alone prevents me from taking the yet stronger step of placing you under arrest. You now stand warned. Attempt no further dictation. I have my own reasons which I will not communicate to anyone, and am alone responsible for the course I have pursued.'

On the face of it, it was a trivial incident. An impudent subordinate had forgotten himself and had been put in his place. But it is impossible to discount the effect which it had on Havelock's mind, already strained with anxiety and a sense of failure. Unconsciously he must have remembered Neill's criticism, which he knew to be unjust, but which, in the particular circumstances, must have rankled there. Havelock was fundamentally a humble man and given to self-criticism. He must have asked himself whether he was to blame for giving up the attempt without at least one more effort. From every military point of view, he was right, but a man's deepest feelings are not always to be assuaged by logic.

He had written on 31st July that he could not attack again without the reinforcement of 1,000 infantry and a battery. Yet, four days later, he set out again across the Ganges with his strength increased only by 220 infantry of the 84th Foot and half a battery. Forbes writes:

> 'The first advance had been a forlorn hope; this one differed in that it was forlorn of any hope.'

His total strength was now about 1,400 men. The enemy must have increased rather than diminished in numbers, and he knew that the mutiny at Dinapore had destroyed the chance of any substantial reinforcement for some time, and that the Gwalior contingent were still threatening. His decision to renew his advance was a bad error of judgement, and one which he would not have made a few years earlier, and it would seem that he was swayed not by his judgement but by his feelings. He believed Lucknow to be on the point of starvation. He was haunted by the memory of Cawnpore, and there must have been in his subconscious mind the feeling that other men besides Neill were blaming him for faint-heartedness. A great general should have been able to put such things out of his mind, but a great general must always have something a little insensitive about him, and age and the strain of many campaigns wear out the strongest of men. If it was a failure of judgement, it was a very human one, and one in which he was risking his reputation and his life.

It is ironical to find the fire-eating Neill, only three days after writing his letter calling for action, urging delay on account of his own danger. His actions during those days were inconsistent with the bold course which he was urging on his superior. On 25th July, the day on which he had taken over command at Cawnpore, he was telegraphing to Grant, 'All well here. I will hold my own against any odds.' In his journal for 31st July, he boasts, 'If the 42nd (Native) are within reach, I will deal them a blow that will astound them.' On 4th August, he discovered that the 42nd were in fact within reach, and his tune changed abruptly, for he wrote to Havelock and begged him to delay his departure until he had dispersed a party of mutineers who were collecting at Bithur. Havelock reported to Grant:

> 'When I finally advanced, resolving if possible to win, General Neill sent me the most pressing representations regarding his danger from the Saugor troops.'

(The Saugor troops were, as it happened the 42nd Native Infantry.)

A few days later, Neill telegraphed to Grant:

> 'Nothing can be done toward Lucknow from here till reinforced. Any advance now with reduced numbers and those seriously weakened with disease, exposure and fatigue would be madness.'

Havelock naturally ignored Neill's plea. On August 4th the brigade marched out again, little more than 1,400 strong, and on the 5th they were in action again at Busherat-Gange. It was a scrambling, inconclusive fight at the end of which the enemy retired in no great haste, carrying off with them all their artillery except for two small guns. 'The whole day's work', Tytler wrote, 'was unsatisfactory, only two small guns, formerly captured by us, and, as we thought, destroyed, being taken.' The British casualties were only two killed and 23 wounded, but cholera was among them again and, when they found that the enemy had taken up a new defensive position a few miles back, the brigade was in no shape for another effort.

Nothing is more significant of the change which age and weariness had wrought in Havelock than the fact that at this juncture he summoned a council of war to debate their next move. He had never been a believer in what, in happier days, he had scornfully called 'Jackdaws' Parliaments'. He must have remembered those interminable discussions at Jalalabad with Sale vacillating and Broadfoot fulminating, while he, as a junior officer, sat silent and critical. It was the first time in his career that he had formally consulted his officers before making up his mind.

Even so there was still much of the old Havelock in him. He limited the council to what he called, 'the only three staff officers in my force whom I ever consult confidentially', Tytler, Crommelin, his Chief Engineer and his son, Henry; and, though he asked them for their opinions he seems to have already formed his own. Tytler and Crommelin were at one in urging that any further advance must be costly and might well be disastrous. Henry, with the fire and impetuosity of youth, pleaded for one more effort. Henry wrote afterwards:

> 'The fact is that I voted for advancing at all hazards. Tytler and Crommelin, Tytler especially, took me to task severely about this, saying that I was prepared to sacrifice the whole force and the interests of British India, rather than compromise my father's and my own reputation by a retreat. Tytler particularly urged, "You must recollect that this is more than a personal question. However galling it is to the General and you to retire, you must have regard to the interests of the Government." Crommelin agreed with him strongly and my father then said, "I agree with Tytler."'

It was the only possible end to an attempt which should never have been made, and Havelock knew it before he consulted his officers.

The enemy were pressing on his rear and might molest his crossing and he determined to teach them one last lesson. Weary and heartsick though he was, he was still as full of fight as a wounded lion and he turned suddenly and savagely on his pursuers and routed them in front of Mungulwar, capturing several guns and sending the Sepoys scurrying headlong up the causeway. They left not only the guns but 200 dead behind them, while the British casualties amounted in all to no more than thirty.

On the 13th, the day after the fight, the crossing began. Crommelin had made shift to provide a more permanent bridge than the boats and all that day the column straggled across the bridge, the men marching anyhow, with eyes on the ground and dragging steps. The General sat on his horse by the riverside and watched for hour after hour, as his last hope faded and the sullen, tired army crawled back to its lair.

In Lucknow, Colonel McLeod Innes was one of those who waited in lessening hope for the sound of British guns to the south of them, till they learned from spies that the British column had re-crossed the Ganges. They thought themselves to be near to starvation, their numbers were decreasing daily by gunfire and disease and they were kept perpetually on the alert by the investing force's mining operations. If any criticism of Havelock's action were justifiable, it would have been from such as they, in the bitterness of hope deferred. Unlike Neill, Innes was a gentleman and a generous man, and his opinion is worth quoting.

> 'To face the enormous force collected against him with the strength of only an ordinary battalion, at 600 miles from his base, with his communications interrupted, and to retire successfully to Cawnpore, as he did on August 13th, was a feat that seems to throw into the shade the most brilliant and audacious deeds of the vaunted days of Wellesley and Lake. The intense sorrow with which Havelock made up his mind to this withdrawal may easily be imagined, but as a military measure, it was imperatively necessary.'

Havelock had telegraphed to the C.-in-C.:

> 'I must prepare your Excellency's mind for my abandonment, with great grief and reluctance, of the hope of relieving Lucknow.'

By nightfall of the 13th, the last man and the last gun had crossed the Ganges, and he rode alone to his quarters in Cawnpore. Of his 1,400 fighting men, 335 were disabled by sickness or wounds, and that night his chief surgeon reported that if the same ratio of casualties continued, in six weeks there would be no men left.

The mutineers at Bithur still threatened and were now 4,000 strong. Havelock was never one to await a threat if there was another way of meeting it, and on the 16th he marched out with all the fit men whom he could collect and fell on them before they knew that he had started. The Sepoys fought fiercely, but for once Havelock had the heavier artillery and Olphert's and Maude's guns blasted them while the infantry drove at them from both flanks with the bayonet. The Madras Fusiliers crossed bayonets with the 42nd Native Foot—the regiment of whom Neill had been going to make such short work—and had much ado to drive them out of their trenches. At the end of a hard-fought day, the enemy broke and ran, leaving 250 dead and two guns. The British had lost over fifty men, whom they could ill afford to spare, and twelve more had fallen by sunstroke.

On the day on which Havelock fought at Cawnpore, Sir Colin Campbell, who had arrived in India on the 13th, took over command of the army. Havelock had already telegraphed to him in terms which made perfectly clear that, whatever mischances he had suffered, he had not lost his will to fight nor his determination to reach Lucknow.

> 'I am ready to fight anything [his message ended], but the above are great odds, and a battle lost here would do the State infinite damage. I solicit your Excellency to send me reinforcements. I can then assume the initiative, march to Lucknow, to Agra, to Delhi, wherever my services may be required. With 2,000 British soldiers, nothing could stand before us and our powerful artillery. I shall soon have equipped eighteen guns, six of siege calibre. But I want artillerymen and officers.'

Campbell's reply made it equally clear that he at any rate appreciated the magnitude of Havelock's achievement. He wrote:

> 'I received your despatches by telegraph of the 12th inst. and the 6th inst., reporting the successful results of the attacks made on the enemy by the force under your command, of those days respectively. The sustained energy, promptitude and vigorous action by which your whole proceedings have been marked, during the late operations, deserve the highest praise

and it will be a most agreeable duty to me to make known to his Lordship, the Governor-General, the sense I entertain of the able manner in which you have carried out the instructions of Sir Patrick Grant.'

Such words from a soldier like Campbell were worth the having and must have heartened Havelock, who had had little of praise or gratitude lately. But they must have made more severe the shock when, on returning from the expedition to Bithur, he picked up a copy of the *Gazette* and learned from it that he had been superseded in his command by Sir James Outram. There had been no official despatch notifying him of the impending change and it was a hard way to learn of it.

There has never been any suggestion that the slight was intentional. Neither Grant nor Campbell was of the type who could contemplate such a grave discourtesy, and it was obviously the result of an oversight at Headquarters at Calcutta. In the stress of Grant's departure and Campbell's arrival it would be an easy matter for the staff of either of them to think that the other had dealt with it. But there was an impression in India at the time that the supersession was a mark of the Government's displeasure at the double failure to reach Lucknow. Many senior officers felt that he had been hardly treated, but there is no trace in any of his printed writings that he shared the view. If he complained at all, it must have been in a private letter to his wife, which she quite rightly kept to herself, but, as a matter of fact, he seems to have taken the supersession quite calmly and not to have resented it. He was too old a soldier to repine at what was a very common occurrence in army life. He had superseded Neill, now it was his turn. Few men escaped the fate sooner or later. Even Sir Arthur Wellesley had been rewarded for the victory of Vimiero by being twice passed over in favour of two senile nonentities. Any non-purchase officer like Havelock had to learn to accept supersession as a matter of course. In any case, if he had troubled his head about it he could have felt happy in the fact that he had not technically been superseded at all, since Outram had been appointed to command the Cawnpore and Dinapore divisional district, an appointment which had been vacant since Wheeler's death at Cawnpore, and one which Havelock had never held. It involved command of all British troops operating in the district and therefore of Havelock's column.

The most important thing was that he was being succeeded by Sir James Outram, an old colleague and a man under whom any officer in the army would have been proud to serve. On the day of his return from Bithur Havelock published the last of his magniloquent Orders of the Day—the last and the most moving. Though the style is still somewhat Napoleonic, his passionate sincerity illuminates the last passages of it:

> 'And if conquest can now be attained under the most trying circumstances, what will be the triumph and retribution of the time when the armies from China, from the Cape and from England shall sweep through the land? Soldiers! In that moment your privations, your sufferings, and your valour will not be forgotten by a grateful country. You will be acknowledged to have been the stay and prop of British India in the time of her severest trial.'

CHAPTER XXII

ALUM BAGH (1857)

THERE WAS still much of the old Havelock in him. At Jalalabad, fifteen years before, he had surveyed the deficiencies of the defending force and demanded guns, mortars and a chaplain. He was still in command at Cawnpore until Outram could arrive and he found that there was no chaplain, since the last had been murdered with Wheeler's garrison. This was a more than ever urgent need, since so many of his brigade were in hospital and sadly often there were funerals to be taken. Mr. Robert Clare Tucker, who was in charge at Benares, offered to send a Baptist chaplain from the mission there, though an ignorant native clerk substituted the word 'Papist' for 'Baptist'. Havelock, a Baptist himself, was no great sectarian and there were many Roman Catholics among the Irishmen in the Madras Fusiliers and among the 78th Highlanders, so he accepted but, on inviting the new chaplain to breakfast on his arrival, found that he was entertaining a minister of his own denomination, instead of the Roman priest whom he had expected.

Reinforcements to the temporal arm were a more pressing matter. The total strength of his command, according to the muster rolls, was 1,700, but he could not count on more than about 650 for active employment. Outram had arrived at Dinapore but was held up there by the need to deal with the situation presented by the recent mutiny of the garrison and by the swarms of mutinous troops who beset the road over which the troops must travel to reach Cawnpore. The 5th Fusiliers and the 90th Rifles were available, but there was delay in sending them on to Allahabad and a further delay when they arrived there. Campbell had taken command at Calcutta, relieving Grant, who wrote a charming farewell letter to Havelock, congratulating him on a 'wise military discretion' in his retirement from Oudh and thanking him for his 'invaluable service'. In his first report to Campbell, Havelock laid clearly before him the parlous state of his brigade and the vital need of reinforcement, adding, for greater emphasis:

> 'If I do not get any promise of reinforcement from Your Excellency by return of telegraph, I must retire at once to Allahabad. I have no longer here a defensible entrenchment; that on the river being taken in reverse by the enemy now assembling on the right bank of the Ganges . . . sickness continues to thin our ranks; we lose men by cholera to the number of five or six daily.'

After a detailed account of his own strength and that of the enemy forces who were threatening him, he reverted to his possible further retreat:

> 'I may be attacked from Gwalior by the mutinous contingent, with 5,000 men and 30 guns, or by the large forces which are assembling at Farrukhabad under its rebellious Nuwaub, which has also a formidable artillery. But, as they can hardly unite, I can defeat either or both in successive fights. But, if reinforcements cannot be sent to me, I see no alternative but abandoning for a time the advantages which I have gained in this part of India and retiring on Allahabad, where everything can be organised for a triumphant advance in the cold season.'

There was some criticism of this despatch by officers who did not scruple to say that Havelock had lost his nerve and was developing a taste for retirements, but it was unfair and malicious. All that he asked for was enough to bring his strength up to 2,000 or 2,500 men, with whom, as he wrote, 'I can hold this place with a high hand.' A man who has lost his nerve does not calmly contemplate the prospect of fighting in succession two armies each of which outnumbers him in men and guns. He was blamed for mentioning a possible retirement to Allahabad, but it was a danger and not a remote one if he could not be reinforced, and he had never shirked the telling of facts because they were unpleasant or because he might be blamed for it.

He was stating what was the plain fact. He had at the moment 685 effectives. The enemy had two armies each of about 5,000 men. If he could bring his strength up to 2,000—less than half the strength of one of the opposing forces—he would fight them both, one after another. If not, he would retreat rather than sacrifice his whole force. That was the situation as he saw it and that was what he told his superior, who cordially agreed with him. Campbell was a man of great determination and energy and he bent all of it to the task of reinforcing Cawnpore. The 5th and the 90th were given orders to use all speed in their advance, and Headquarters and seven companies of the 90th were put on board river steamers for quick passage up the Ganges, while a battalion of Madras Infantry and a 6-pounder battery were to follow by road.

There was a further irritating delay when the first detachments reached Allahabad, where the Commandant took the responsibility of disembarking them for the protection of his own district. Mutineers were said to be hovering in the neighbourhood and the Commandant thought himself justified in using his own initiative. Havelock thought otherwise and a furious telegram forbade him to detain them

> 'not for an hour, for any purpose whatever. Push them on with all speed. I will not permit the troops of this column being diverted to the purpose of casual operations by the officers under my command.'

The Commandant apparently did not know Havelock or possibly thought that now it was safe to defy him, for he sent a long message urging the importance of the movements which he was proposing to carry out. He found, as Neill had found, that it was not advisable to take too many liberties with General Havelock. A second telegram told him:

> 'Whatever may be your opinion of the probable success of your operations against the Dinapore mutineers and its consequences, I consider I am the best judge how the reinforcements sent to me by the C.-in-C. are to be employed, and I desire that they may be pushed forward without any delay or further remonstrance or remark.'

There was no more delay. Havelock was still in command at Cawnpore, and as long as he commanded he meant to have his orders obeyed. He was still bent on the relief of Lucknow even if he were not to have the task of carrying it out.

His determination was further strengthened by a letter from Inglis, which he received on 23rd August seven days after it had been sent. Inglis wrote almost desperately of his situation. 'We have only a small force,' he wrote in reply to an earlier suggestion that he should attempt to cut himself out of the city,

> '. . . You must bear in mind how I am hampered; that I have upwards of 120 sick and wounded and at least 220 women and about 230 children and no carriage of any description. . . . In consequence of the news received, I shall soon put this force on half rations. Our provisions will then last us till about the 10th of September. If you hope to save this force, no time must be lost in pushing forward. We are daily being attacked by the enemy who are within a few yards of our defences. . . . Our native force, having been assured, on Colonel Tytler's authority, of your near approach, some twenty-five days ago, are naturally losing confidence and, if they leave us, I do not see how our defences are to be manned. . . .'

Inglis was in an extremely unpleasant position and Havelock of course could not know that he had miscalculated his stores, nor that he was unduly afraid of the loyalty of the native troops in the garrison, whose conduct had been and remained admirable throughout. He was not in a position to make any promise of speedy relief and he answered:

> 'My dear Colonel,
>
> 'I have your letter of the 16th. I can only say, hold on, and do not negotiate, but rather perish, sword in hand. Sir Colin Campbell, who came out at a day's notice to command, on the news arriving of General Anson's death, promises me fresh troops and you will be my first care. The reinforcements may reach me in from twenty to twenty-five days and I will prepare everything for a march on Lucknow.'

It was perhaps cold comfort to the garrison, eating their half-rations among well-stocked storehouses, and to their commander looking askance at his loyal natives, but the advice not to negotiate was sound and based on a lifetime of experience. The garrison of Kabul had negotiated with Dost Mohammed, as the garrison of Cawnpore had with the Nana Sahib, and Havelock had seen the results of both attempts. His exhortation to perish sword in hand was not as vainglorious as it sounded, since to negotiate with native power was only a quicker and viler way to destruction. He heard no more from Inglis until 8th September, when he received a letter dated the 1st, which emphasised the straits to which the garrison were reduced and gave the 21st as the last day of possible resistance.

Outram was on his way, though his progress was slower than either of them had anticipated, since he met with resistance at many points on his route and had to fight. The fact that Outram was coming to join him at Cawnpore was a great relief to Havelock, because at first Outram and Campbell had conceived the idea of the relief force marching to Lucknow by another route, leaving Havelock to force his own way across the Ganges and through Aong and Busherat-Gange to join him before the city. To this plan Havelock had strenuously objected. He knew that he could make little progress with what troops he had and, master of tactics that he was, he saw the folly of operating two separate and comparatively weak forces, when they might be combined into strength; it would be hardly less foolish to abandon Cawnpore as an advanced base for the move on Lucknow. Outram seems to have formed an exaggerated idea of the amount of flooding in the country between Cawnpore and Lucknow and to have believed that another route would make for quicker movement. Fortunately Havelock's expert knowledge of the country prevailed and Outram arrived in Cawnpore on 15th September, bringing with him the main body of the reinforcements. They were strong in infantry and guns now, but Outram had no cavalry with him. The nearest were at Delhi, where the 9th Lancers were already engaged, but by strenuous efforts during the last month Havelock had managed to raise the numbers of his volunteer Horse to 109, who were increased by another forty when a Lieutenant Johnson arrived with an unexpected reinforcement. At the same time, he had been busily reconnoitring the Ganges for a place suitable for building a permanent bridge. Crommelin had constructed two floating bridges and Havelock chose a place where islands in the river made it easy to convert the two into one bridge with the islands to link them up. In the middle of all this activity he still found time to deal with two officers who were reported to have entered a native temple and caused scandal to its congregation of believers, and he issued an order warning the troops against any similar act of sacrilege in either Hindu or Moslem precincts. He was a respecter of the faith of all true believers and, for all his upbringing and habit, a tolerant man. 'We must not imitate these wretches', he wrote in his order.

In every way he was making ready for Outram's coming and for the next advance and, as soon as the road to Allahabad was reported safe, he gladly sent off a convoy of his sick and wounded to the hospital, where they would get far better attention than was possible in the makeshift buildings at Cawnpore.

There were a thousand other details to attend to and the amount of work which he got through is astonishing. There were boats to collect for helping in the crossing, to which he added the prudent step of providing several barges to be taken with the force for later crossing of the Sai and the Gumti nearer to Lucknow, together with ox-waggons for their transport on the line of march. There was a provisional division of the force into two wings for the march and a small body to remain at Cawnpore, all of which had to be submitted to Outram for his approval. The approval was forthcoming except that Outram decided that the wings were to be re-christened brigades, an alteration which pleased him and gave no particular trouble to anybody, or any increased efficiency to the force. Perhaps Havelock had overlooked the fact that Outram was a Major-General and that the brigade had now become a division. It is not a matter which would have struck him as very important.

If we can believe Neill's diary—which is never certain—his advice was put freely at Havelock's disposal all through this month. Once he records that 'General Havelock seemed displeased with me'. That at any rate we can believe without difficulty.

When Outram arrived at last on 15th September, Havelock greeted him most cordially. They had been friends for many years and had last seen each other a few months before in Persia. Outram genuinely admired the achievements of the last weeks and at once sought to give the strongest and most public possible proof of his confidence in his old colleague and second-in-command. On the day after his arrival he published the famous order which aroused so much admiration and won for him from Campbell the name of 'The Bayard of India'.

> 'The important duty of relieving Lucknow [it ran] had been first entrusted to Brigadier-General Havelock; and Major-General Outram feels that it is due to that distinguished officer and to the noble and strenuous exertions which he has already made to achieve that object, that to him should accrue the honour of that achievement. Major-General Outram is confident that the great end for which Brigadier-General Havelock and his brave troops have so long and so gloriously fought, will now, under the blessing of Providence, be accomplished. The Major-General therefore, in gratitude for and admiration of the brilliant deed of arm achieved by Brigadier-General Havelock and his gallant troops, will cheerfully waive his rank in favour of that officer on this occasion, and will accompany the force to Lucknow in his civil capacity, tendering his military services to Brigadier-General Havelock as a volunteer. On the relief of Lucknow the Major-General will resume his position at the head of the force.'

Havelock's formal acknowledgement was made with his usual modesty and grace, but it may be wondered whether he was really grateful for this singular way of showing gratitude and esteem. No one knowing Outram's generous character could think that he meant it in any but the most complimentary sense and its publication caused a storm of approval in India. But the approval was for him and not for Havelock and, though genuine in intention, it was essentially unfair, as such extravagant gestures always are.

On 19th September Crommelin's bridge was ready, and the division began its crossing. Neill commanded the First Infantry Brigade, which included the Madras Fusiliers, the 5th Fusiliers, the 84th and two companies of the 64th. Colonel Hamilton of the 78th Highlanders commanded the Second Brigade, comprising the 78th, the 90th Rifles and Brayser's Sikhs. The artillery, under Major Cooper, consisted of three batteries, Maude's and Eyre's 18-pounders, and another battery under Olphert, who was affectionately, and for excellent reasons, known to his men as 'Hell-fire Jack'. The cavalry under Barrow now numbered

150, including Johnson's irregulars. The mutineers threw away their best chance at the start when they made no serious attempt to interfere with the division's crossing of the Ganges. Even with Crommelin's new bridge it was a long and perilous operation, and the mutineers had more than enough strength to have made it a costly and difficult one. But they had had recent experience of Havelock as an enemy and only offered a slight resistance, retiring hastily on to their main body which was occupying an entrenched position in front of Mungulwar. They could hardly have chosen a worse position and nothing, it would seem, could cure them of the belief that the British would always attack from the front. They had overlooked the fact that Havelock's advanced base had been at Mungulwar and that he knew every inch of the surrounding ground, with the result that in a very short time they found the British infantry closing in on their flank and rear while the new weight of the artillery battered them in front. They then had the causeway which divided the marshes to cross, and what might have proved a tactical asset to them became a nightmare road down which they fled with the British cavalry in pursuit. For the first time since they had started from Allahabad, Havelock had enough cavalry to turn a retreat into a rout, since on that narrow path the enemy were packed close together and a squadron could chase them as well as could a brigade in open country. The pursuit swept into and through Busherat-Gange, where the brigade had fought so hard in their last advance, and where now the cavalry rode over and captured two guns which had come into action against them behind an entrenchment. The infantry, hampered by the rain which continued to pour down in torrents, came up too late for any further advance that day, and the division spent the night in cheerless bivouac on ground only too familiar to some of them. The second day's advance should have been more difficult had the Sepoys used their natural advantages. The path led them to Bunni on the River Sai, on the far bank of which were strong gun-emplacements whose function was to protect the bridge which formed the only crossing and which could have easily been destroyed by a retreating force. But the Sepoys were in too much of a hurry to get away from Havelock Sahib and they had abandoned the emplacement, after throwing the guns into the river, and made no attempt to destroy the bridge.

The column, hardly able to believe their good fortune, trudged on through the driving rain. The mud clung to their feet and the steamy heat drenched them in sweat and made the weight of their weapons and kit a weary burden, but no shot was fired at them, no long-distance gun opened up, there was no sight or sound of an enemy: nothing but the rumble of the gun-wheels, the splashing and slipping of the cavalry horses and the wracking sound of their own breathing, till towards mid-day, just as they halted, they heard the sound of guns in the far distance, a muffled and persistent drumming, and knew that at last they were hearing the guns at Lucknow.

Havelock ordered a halt and the tired infantry turned off the road, flung themselves down on the soaking grass and searched in their haversacks for meat and biscuit, since none of them knew how soon they might have to move on again. As they ate and rested, they saw that preparations were going forward for some incomprehensible move, for the batteries were passing through them and unlimbering on either side of the road. The soldiers cursed wearily, thinking that the General might have let them get a bit of food before he started another fight, and asking themselves, perhaps, whom he was going to fight in that apparently empty plain. They watched in amazement as the batteries took up their alignment and then they heard with incredulity the order given for the firing of a royal salute. One after another, at their proper intervals, the guns fired and Havelock sat on his horse in rear of them with Outram beside him and his Staff behind. He was staring through the driving rain as though he could see that distant and hard-pressed force in the Residency, as his artillery roared their answer to the garrison's last appeal for help. Then the infantry understood what the message was which the guns were sending and they leaped to their feet and added the sound of their cheers to the roar of the guns.

The sound died away and again there was nothing but the drumming of the rain. Later they learned that no sound of their greeting had reached Lucknow, where the garrison still fought on with undiminished courage and vanishing hope. The infantrymen felt that they were in touch with their comrades and turned with a better relish to their meal. They had horses for a few of the guns now and the drivers brought up their teams, hooked in, and drew the guns back to their place in the column, while the cavalry trotted forward up the track towards the rising ground which lay in front.

It was still early afternoon when the cavalry drew rein on the higher ground and looked downwards towards Lucknow, just visible in the distance, and to the pleasure grounds of the Alum Bagh nearer at hand. One of them made a signal to the main body and in a few moments Colonel Tytler was galloping forward to join them. The infantry had finished their meal and were taking what rest they could while they had time for it. Tytler came thundering back along the track, the water flying in great splashes from beneath his horse's hoofs and behind him the cavalry followed more leisurely as a few puffs of white smoke appeared above the rise where the enemy guns were searching for the range. The infantry reached for their rifles and began to pull on their sodden equipment. A spare, white-haired figure in a blue frock-coat trotted up the road on an arab charger and the bugles blew for the advance.

CHAPTER XXIII

THE RESIDENCY (1857)

IT WAS the first time that the bugles had sounded since the division had crossed the Ganges. The mutineers knew all the British bugle-calls, which were the same as those used in the native regiments, and Havelock had silenced his bugles for security. But now there was no need for further concealment. The enemy stood to fight before Lucknow, and the British came down the hill like hounds running into their fox. The Alum Bagh, the old pleasure gardens of the Begums of Oudh, lay beside the trunk road and about four miles short of the city. Once the wives of the Kings of Oudh had walked there beneath the jasmine and hibiscus and sat to watch the play of goldfish in the marble basins. Now the scarlet and white beneath the trees was the uniform of the mutinous regiments and the sun struck flashes from the brass of the guns and the steel bayonets. There were 12,000 Sepoys in position across the road with their left flank in the Alum Bagh and their right resting on the protection of a swamp. The incessant rain of the past few weeks had reduced the whole countryside to little better than a morass and floods covered the whole front of the enemy position. Their big guns were already in action as the British came over the rise but they were doing little damage and Havelock pushed his own guns forward and engaged them as the infantry deployed. For the first time since the beginning of the campaign the Sepoys felt the full weight of British artillery, which outnumbered their own and which was handled with a reckless courage which took them by surprise. 'Hell-fire Jack' took his battery forward at the gallop, plunged with them through a brimming ditch, swung to the left and opened fire at short range.

The Sepoys had put their trust in the marsh which protected their right flank, forgetting—as the French, when they had faced Marlborough in the Low Countries, had forgotten—that a marsh is no protection unless it is quite impassable or completely covered by fire. Havelock was adopting his favourite turning movement, since it had never failed him against native troops and, since they were strongest on their centre and left and had trusted their right flank to the protection of Nature, he ordered his attack against the right, marsh or no marsh. The first brigade, Neill's, remained on the road and the second, under Hamilton, moved from their position in rear of the first and deployed on the left of the road. The men waded knee-deep, sometimes chest-deep, but they came on without a pause, and, as soon as the attack began to develop, Havelock sent the first brigade against the centre. It would have been a murderous business but for the fire of the British artillery which concentrated on the Alum Bagh, subduing the defending guns and destroying the infantry as they began to change front to meet the attack on their right.

Havelock's instinct or experience had guided him shrewdly about the passage of the marsh, and the infantry went through it so fast that he sent Olphert with his horse battery after them to give them support. The mutineers found themselves attacked simultaneously in front and on the flank. Eyre's and Maude's batteries blasted their front, and on their right the 78th and the 90th came steadily on with the help of Olphert's. Almost at the same moment the two attacks reached the Alum Bagh, as Neill's men swarmed over the defences in front and the 78th burst in on the flank. The Sepoys broke and ran in a disorderly mob, huddled together on the Trunk Road, and the gunners raised their sights and poured everything that they had into that packed and slow-moving target where the road was jammed with waggons, guns, horses and men. Then Havelock gave an order to the cavalry and Barrow swept forward to take up the pursuit. The mutineers were panic-stricken and the cavalry rode into them and over them and among them, sabring them as they went, until they were almost under the walls of the city.

There Barrow checked them, as the mutineers struggled and fought to be the first to cross the bridge which crossed the canal at the Char Bagh, on the boundary of the city and a bare two miles from the Residency position, where the garrison had heard, with excitement and thankfulness, the cannonade of the battle. The little band of horsemen, who had done such destruction during the last days, wheeled about and walked their horses back along the Lucknow road towards the infantry. As they did so, a mounted man galloped up the road to meet them and handed a despatch to Outram. The infantry, reforming in the gardens, the gunners withdrawing their guns, looked across the swampy fields towards the road and saw that Outram was galloping back on his huge Waler and waving a paper over his head. As he passed, he shouted to them that Delhi had been taken.

The capture of the Alum Bagh removed the last obstacle in the way of the British before Lucknow, but the city itself was a formidable position. The relieving force lay that night to the south of it, some four miles from the nearest point and six from the Residency. Lucknow is surrounded by water, with the River Gumti to the north and the canal, which branches off from it to the east and rejoins it on the west, completing the circuit. At that date there were three principal bridges which could be used by an entering force—the Char Bagh Bridge on the south, crossed by the road from the Alum Bagh, a smaller bridge on the east where the road from Dilkusha enters the city, and, crossing the Gumti on the north side, the Iron Bridge, which was close to the Residency position. The garrison were concentrated in the Residency buildings at the north of the enceinte and the rest of the city was in native hands, so that Havelock's division would have to fight their way not only into Lucknow but, whichever way they chose, through a district of streets and houses. The enemy were more than 20,000 strong with guns enough to cover all approaches, so that they could easily contain the garrison in their buildings and yet spare the greater part of their numbers for resisting entry by a force from outside. With their compact and concentrated position they could move men and guns rapidly from side to side of the city to strengthen any threatened point. Both Havelock, who did not know the interior of the city, and Outram, who knew it well, realised the magnitude of the task which faced them. Havelock decided to give his men a full day's rest before trying to force an entry. It was the plainest wisdom, but the garrison, hearing no sound from the guns after the cannonading of the day before, began to wonder whether, at the last moment their hopes were again to be disappointed. It was not till nightfall that a native messenger from the division succeeded in reaching the Residency, telling them that the assault would be made on the 25th.

All day, on the 24th, the division took their rest, while Havelock and Outram debated the plan of assault, and it was now that the first unhappy results of a divided command appeared. Outram, while technically still Havelock's willing subordinate, exerted steady pressure to get his own plan accepted, instead of the plan which Havelock had sketched out and now urged upon him.

There were three possible points of entry at the three bridges which crossed either the river or the canal. Havelock, profound believer as ever in turning movements, had at once chosen the furthest point, which would give his division a long march over open country but would bring them, probably without fighting at all, to the Iron Bridge on the north. Having once forced that, they would be almost able to reach out and touch the hands of the garrison in the Residency. Outram strongly opposed the plan, on account of the state of the ground, which he held to be so badly flooded that it would be impossible to move the heavy guns and difficult to move even the lighter horse-guns.

Havelock, as might be expected, had not overlooked that problem, but he had had recent experience of crossing marshes which others had held to be impassable, and he was ready, if need be, to sacrifice the help of his heavy guns for the sake of the best tactical route. The Iron Bridge, where he hoped to cross the River Gumti, was so near to the Residency that his advance might be helped by a well-timed sortie of the garrison, but this was a plan which Outram mistrusted. When the division had left Cawnpore he had written to warn Inglis against any rash attempt at a sortie and again he wrote from the Alum Bagh.

> 'It may be late before we reach you, don't risk any sally from your post that might expose your position to assault.'

Outram, though he had resigned the command, opposed Havelock's first choice of route, even though it would have taken them through undefended country and given them at the end the very minimum of street-fighting. In such a position it is impossible to say that either was absolutely right. If the ground were really as badly flooded as Outram thought, the advance might have been seriously delayed and deprived of the help of even the lighter guns, but, if it were passable at all, it would bring them into the city at a far better place than any other possible way.

The second route was the direct road over the Char Bagh Bridge and through the city, and neither of them gave it more than a moment's consideration, since it would involve at least a mile and a half of fighting in the streets, where the advantage would be wholly with the defence. The third was a compromise between the other two and was the route on which they finally decided. It involved forcing the Char Bagh Bridge, then turning to right and following the line of the canal until they had passed the point where it was crossed by the road from Dilkusha, later changing direction to the left, at a building and garden called the Secundra Bagh, and fighting their way past the old palaces, the Kaiser Bagh and the Chutter Munzil. It was not an ideal way and much depended on the state of the defence in the palaces. In any case there would be a thousand yards or more of street-fighting at the Residency end of it before they could reach the Bailey Guard, the eastern bastion of the defence. Havelock was in an unhappy position. Technically he was in command, but Outram was insistent on his own plan. It would be difficult and embarrassing to Havelock to withstand him, especially as in the last resort Outram could announce his resumption of command. Havelock still believed that the circuitous route was the only sensible one, even at the cost of some delay, and, if he had known the true state of the stores in the Residency, he might have insisted. As it was, they both believed that the garrison were at the point of starvation and in that case it was always possible that Inglis's native troops, of whom he was suspicious, might lose heart and turn against him. So Havelock accepted Outram's plan, not without misgiving and prepared his orders for the next day.

The column of attack was to be led by Neill's brigade, supported by Maude with his battery, and their first task was to carry the Char Bagh Bridge, which was heavily defended and covered by the fire of guns sited in a temple on the further bank. As soon as this was taken and the guns silenced, the division would cross over and take the road to the right, leaving a battalion and some attached troops to hold the bridge until the main body had reached the Secundra Bagh, after which they would rejoin the main body. The bugles blew reveille in the dawn of a rainy day, but before that Havelock was astir and on his knees in his tent, commending his cause and his soul to God. The column began to move at 8.30, the 5th Fusiliers leading Neill's brigade, and they were under fire before nine o'clock from a few guns which the mutineers had left in a building called the Yellow House, on the right of the road. Maude's battery soon silenced them and the Fusiliers marched on to a bend in the road where they came under direct fire from the bridge at a range of 200 yards. The fire was intense and for a time they could make no progress. The mutineers had a battery of six guns, one of them a 24-pounder, on the Lucknow bank, and the high buildings in rear of them were full of riflemen. Outram was riding with the leading files, while Havelock's Divisional Headquarters were at the head of the second brigade and still on the Alum Bagh road. Outram rode off to the right with a small party to look for a position from which they could enfilade the enemy battery, but they could find nothing and the only course open to them was to carry the bridge by a frontal attack.

At this point of the battle it is difficult to find a coherent account, or even any account which agrees with any other. Most of the officers who afterwards described the action were hotly engaged in it and necessarily prevented from seeing much more than their own little corner of the scene. As often happens when battles are recounted, many of them are concerned to make the facts fit in with their pre-conceived opinions about a man or a regiment. Marshman, a whole-hearted partisan of the Havelock family, gives an account of the storming of the bridge which gives all the credit to young Henry Havelock, an account which Maude denies and Willis, who commanded the 84th, does not mention. According to Marshman, Henry Havelock, seeing the infantry held up and reluctant to advance across the bridge, spoke to Neill and asked him if he would order an assault, to which Neill replied that he was not in command 'and would not take the responsibility'. Henry then turned his horse and galloped back along the side of the column to get instructions from his father. He returned, after what Marshman calls a 'suspiciously short time', to tell Neill that he was ordered to attack, and himself headed the charge with Colonel Tytler, who was wounded. But Marshman was not a soldier and had to rely on second-hand information, besides being more of a partisan than a historian. Maude, who was at the bridge, denies the story about Henry's ride back and return, but says of Neill, 'I have no recollection of seeing him during the whole of the day.' Maude is, as a rule, a reliable story-teller, but he was desperately busy with his battery at the time, as the first discharge from the enemy had wrecked one of his guns and killed and wounded some of the gunners, and he and his subaltern were trying to get another gun into action. He agrees that Tytler rode over the bridge, but says that only his horse was hurt and that he was untouched. He does not believe the story about Henry, whom he did not like, though he admits his courage. The important thing is that the bridge was carried by a determined rush of the Madras Fusiliers, supported by the 5th and the 84th and at last the British were within the walls of Lucknow. This confusion of evidence prevails throughout the rest of the day's fighting and, as is only to be expected, becomes stronger as the day wore on and the fighting became more desperate and more an affair of isolated struggles, as one unit after another were engulfed in the streets. The 78th and some of the Sikhs were left as rearguard at the bridge, while the main body wheeled to the right and began to make their way along the bank of the canal. They were to follow by the same route, but, as it happened, missed their way and did not rejoin the rest until they had reached the streets near the Residency.

It is plain from all the accounts which have survived that the senior officers of the regiments were conscious throughout the day of a lack of control and an absence of orders. Outram was ahead with the advance-guard, and had been wounded at the Char Bagh, when a bullet passed through his arm. His staff urged him to retire to have the wound dressed, but he refused and remained in the saddle all day. 'If I had gone to the rear', he said afterwards, with some lack of modesty, 'we should never have got to the Residency', and, indeed, as a guide he was invaluable since, when he had been Chief Commissioner of Oudh, he had known Lucknow thoroughly. Havelock, until the last assault, was, as he should have been, half-way down the column, where he could control the movements of his reserve battalions. But, by this means, the force was virtually split into two halves, neither of whom really knew who was commanding them. Maude sums it up fairly when he writes:

> 'One is forced to the conclusion that, from a military point of view, an advance was undertaken with an insouciance of which the culpability was only redeemed by the exceeding bravery of the men. It is not pretended that the General of the first brigade (Neill), did anything. The General who actually led us (Outram), had his wits about him and was cool and collected enough; but, having voluntarily subdued his rank, he could not take any independent steps, without involving a grave breach of discipline, while the General (Havelock), who was nominally in command, took no initiative whatever.'

Outram admitted afterwards that he had been wrong in resigning the command.

The division passed along the canal bank without encountering much opposition or suffering many casualties and wheeled left again at the Secundra Bagh. The mutineers, after their invariable habit, had counted on an attack by the British by the most direct frontal route and the diversion took them by surprise. To his relief, Havelock found that the buildings of the Shah Nujif and the Moti Mahul were quite empty and that he was only under fire from guns in the Kaiser Bagh and from distant muskets in the old barracks. He halted the column at the Moti Mahul to give the men a breathing space and to allow the rear-guard to catch them up. The 78th had lost their way and it was late in the afternoon when they arrived, having had an almost unmolested passage. The division was now about 1,100 yards from the Bailey Guard and Outram and Havelock met to plan the final assault. It was unhappily at this point that they came into open dispute. An officer who watched them in the open square under the shadow of the tall buildings has left a description of the two men—Outram sitting on his horse, his arm roughly bandaged and his face smeared with blood: Havelock pacing up and down—his horse had been killed—with short steps, looking irritable and anxious. He was determined to make the assault at once, even though the last charge had to be made down a street where the enemy held all the houses. Outram was in favour of giving the troops a long rest and waiting until all the stragglers should have come in. In their separate reports and correspondence afterwards, there is some doubt as to how long a rest Outram was suggesting. His version suggests that he only contemplated a matter of an hour or two, but Havelock seems to have thought that he meant to wait till the next day before sending in the assault, and to this he would not agree. Their debate became heated and at last Outram urged a delay until Moorsom, a Staff Officer who knew Lucknow, could find a safer way of approach.

He may have been wise, but it is easy to understand Havelock's impatience. Outram had not known, as Havelock and his men had known, the weary marches from the Ganges to Busherat-Gange, the bitter fighting at Unao, the heartbreaking return to Mungulwar and Cawnpore. The Ironsides had come 900 miles and they had only another 1,100 yards to go. Havelock, who knew his men, knew that their blood was up and that nothing could stop them, though they might have to suffer heavily in their passage of the street. He remembered that he was in command and for the first time he exercised it in defiance of Outram. He pointed to the street where the enemy waited behind their walls and said, 'There is the street, we can see what we are in for. We shall get slated but we can get through.' And Outram, losing his temper, answered, 'Then, in God's name, go on.'

In God's name Henry Havelock went on. He and Outram led the column into the street and as soon as they entered it a storm of musket-fire came from the barricaded windows and doors of the houses. Neill was one of the first to fall, shot through the head, and soon Highlanders and Fusiliers were jammed between the houses while the fire rained on them from above. Men stumbled and fell and others trod on them as they pressed forward to take their places. Hell-fire Jack Olpherts had managed, by what contrivance he and his men alone knew, to swing round one of his guns so as to give at any rate some covering fire to the infantry, and though many of them fell, the assault surged up the street till they could see the Bailey Guard-gate, a battered remnant which had been filled in with earth and rubble—and behind it the red coats and bayonets of their comrades of the garrison; and now they could hear the cheering which greeted them. The enemy were firing into their rear, but there was no stopping them and they stood at last close behind the heels of the Generals' horses and before the Bailey Guard. Outram, determined to be the first man to enter, put his Waler at the pile of rubble but it baulked and refused. Willing hands from inside the gate clutched his bridle, strong arms and shoulders from behind urged the struggling horse up the rough obstacle and he was triumphantly the first in, if with something less of dignity than he had expected. (Later he was to try hard to be the last man to leave but was forestalled by Inglis, who stood aside, to let him go out before him, remarking, 'You will allow me, Sir, to have the honour of closing my own door.')

Havelock followed more slowly and on foot. He was so exhausted that he could not drag himself over the stone and rubble, and again helping hands were stretched out. As the short, spare figure stood for a moment poised on top of the mound the cheers rang out inside the fortress and went echoing down the street behind him from the men whom he had led at last, victorious, into Lucknow.

CHAPTER XXIV

PIPES AT LUCKNOW (1857)

IT WAS a relief in nothing but name. Havelock's division had suffered over five hundred casualties in fighting their way into the Residency and the combined British forces were not strong enough to attempt a withdrawal, hampered as they were by the presence of so many women and children. The relieving force had brought no supplies with them except for a few emaciated gun-bullocks and at first there was a danger of famine. But Outram's Chief of Staff, Colonel Napier (afterwards Lord Napier of Magdala), instituted a rigorous search of all the buildings in the position and discovered the forgotten ration stores. Outram had assumed command and the garrison were divided into two brigades, commanded by Havelock and Inglis.

Havelock was disappointed that the regiments which had shared with him the march from Allahabad and the fighting at Cawnpore were not allotted to his brigade, in which his only old comrades were a few companies of the 64th and a small party of Sikhs, but he turned perhaps with relief to the routine duties of a brigadier. He was still in good health, but men who had marched with him remarked on how slowly he moved and how the least exertion tired him. He was sixty-two, and most of those years had been spent strenuously in the East. He was losing weight rapidly too, and found the coarse fare of a besieged town repellent to his jaded appetite and only to be tolerated with the help of some 'excellent sherry' which Mr. Gubbins, the Financial Secretary, sent to him.

In many ways the routine of a defended position must have carried him back to his earlier years. He walked round his posts every morning before going to make his report to Outram, visited the sick in hospital, oversaw the counter-mining preparations and attended to discipline. It was all a little like 'overseeing the shirts and socks of No. 4 Coy of Her Majesty's 13th Foot'. It reminded him at times of Jalalabad and he found that 'he did not starve so easily at 62 as he had at 47'. Perhaps his mind went even farther back, to the sixth-form room at Charterhouse, when he was requested to construct a simple cypher for outgoing messages and produced an amalgam of Latin and French with English words, written in Greek characters.

The summer was over and autumn was passing into winter when at last Campbell's relieving force approached Lucknow. Havelock had spent the months in tranquil and familiar routine without any idea that his name had become a synonym for heroism with the people of England. They had suddenly discovered him after long years of neglect, and he was the most widely acclaimed of all the heroes of the Mutiny. His courage and endurance in the face of tremendous odds and perhaps something about his austere and aloof personality had captured the public mind and raised a clamour for his recognition by his Sovereign. In September he was promoted Major-General and the Queen bestowed on him a Knighthood of the Order of the Bath. Forbes notes that he signed an order as Major-General on November 16th so news of his promotion must have reached him, but the first that he heard about his K.C.B. was from Campbell when he entered Lucknow on 17th November.

The once-famous painting of the meeting of Havelock and Outram with Campbell is almost unknown today, and few if any schoolchildren learn the poem which tells of the girl who heard the Highlanders' pipes as they approached the city. The meeting was in a square which was still under fire, and many of the garrison saw it and noted that Havelock was so weak that he had to be helped across the rough ground on a man's arm. It was on that day that he first heard himself addressed as Sir Henry.

Further honours were in store for him. In December he was made a baronet and Parliament voted him a pension for life of £1,000 a year, but he never knew it, for before the news reached India he was dead. As a last token of respect his country transferred the baronetcy to his son, Henry, and the pension to his wife, and after her death to his son. The great anxiety of all his life had been to make provision for his wife and children after his death, but he did not live to know that at last he had achieved it.

Within a few days of Campbell's arrival, Havelock's failing strength began to give way under an attack of dysentery. He was carried to a tent in some gardens and for a few days lay there, conscious and full of the quiet courage which had always been his. His son, who had been wounded at the Char Bagh Bridge and had not fully recovered, watched beside his bed and on 23rd September, Gubbins, coming to pay a visit, found them together. He wrote:

> 'I was directed to a common soldier's tent. Entering it, I found the General's aide-de-camp, Lieutenant Hargood and his medical attendant, Staff-Surgeon Collinson. They whispered to me in mournful accents the grievous news that Sir Henry was worse and pointed to where he lay. It was in a dhooly which served for a bed. The curtain on my side was down. I found young Havelock seated by the further side upon the ground by his dying father. His wounded arm hung in a sling; but with the other he supplied his father's wants. I saw that speech was impossible and sorrowfully withdrew.'

Sometimes a little flicker of strength returned to him and he could say a few words. Hope Grant, an old colleague who had arrived with Campbell's relief, called to see him, and on asking him how he was, got the answer, 'The hand of death is upon me. God Almighty has seen fit to afflict me for some good purpose of his own.'

Outram too came to take leave of him and heard his confident avowal, 'I have for forty years so ruled my life that when death came I might face it without fear.'

He woke early on the morning of 24th November, knowing that his time had come, and said to his son, 'Come now, and see how a Christian can die.' At half-past nine, without speaking again, he died.

Next morning he was buried in the Alum Bagh. Campbell, Outram, Hamilton and the other senior officers stood with Henry by the grave-side, and behind them were the men of the 78th Highlanders and the Madras Fusiliers, and, by himself, Dick Pearson, his orderly bugler, who had held his General's watch for him and taken the time in so many fights. The pipes of the 78th wailed softly and the Enfield rifles of the firing party rang out. Since the times were troubled and the ground where they left him was still unsafe, the only memorial was the letter H carved on a near-by tree.

Book List

GENERAL

Hansard, Parliamentary Debates
The Army List
Allen's Indian Mail, 1843–1858
Fortescue, *History of The British Army*
Cambridge History of India, 1922
Cambridge Modern History, 1904
etc.

BIOGRAPHIES

Marshman, *Havelock*, 1860
A. Forbes, *Havelock*, 1890
Viscount Mersey, *Viceroys of India*, 1934
J. L. Morison, *Lawrence of Lucknow*, 1934
2nd Viscount Hardinge, *Viscount Hardinge*, 1891
Sir H. S. Cunningham, *Earl Canning*, 1891
Sir W. Butler, *Sir Charles Napier*, 1890
Sir J. Kaye, *Lives of the Indian Officers*, 1867
L. J. Trotter, *Brig.-Gen. John Nicholson*, 1897
L. J. Trotter, *Sir James Outram*, 1902
Sir F. J. Goldsmid, *James Outram*, 1880
A. Forbes, *Sir Colin Campbell*, 1895
L. J. Trotter, *Lord Auckland*, 1893
Sir Leppel Griffin, *Ranjit Singh*, 1892
Major W. Broadfoot, *The Career of Major W. Broadfoot*, 1888
Henry Edwards, *Life of Sir Henry Lawrence*, 1872
Sir W. Hunter, *The Marquess of Dalhousie*, 1890

THE CAMPAIGN OF BURMA

Major J. J. Snodgrass, *Narrative of the Campaign of Burma*, 1827

THE CAMPAIGN IN AFGHANISTAN

Sir Henry Havelock, *Narrative of the War in Afghanistan*, 1840
Sir H. M. Durand, *The First Afghan War and its Causes*, 1879
A. Forbes, *The Afghan Wars*, 1892
Sir J. W. Kaye, *History of the War in Afghanistan*, 1851
Col. G. B. Malleson, *History of Afghanistan*, 1879
Lady Sale, *A Journal of the Disasters in Afghanistan*, 1843

GWALIOR AND SIKH WARS

R. S. Rait, *Memories of Major-Gen. Sir Hugh Gough*, 1860
E. J. Thackwell, *Narrative of the Second Sikh War*, 1857
Col. G. B. Malleson, *Decisive Battles of India*, 1885

THE INDIAN MUTINY

Sir J. W. Kaye, *History of the Sepoy War in India*, 1876
Sir T. R. E. Holmes, *History of the Indian Mutiny*, 1883
Col. G. B. Malleson, *History of the Indian Mutiny*, 1880
W. H. Fitchett, *Tales of the Great Mutiny*, 1901
G. Dangerfield, *History of the Indian Mutiny*, 1933
Sir G. O. Trevelyan, *Cawnpore*, 1886
Earl Roberts, *Forty-one Years in India*, 1897
Earl Roberts, *Letters written during the Indian Mutiny*, 1924
M. R. Gubbins, *An Account of the Mutinies in Oudh*, 1858
Col. F. C. Maude and J. W. Sherer, *Memories of the Mutiny*, 1894
Major-Gen. Sir T. Seaton, *From Cadet to Colonel*, 1866
Lt.-Gen. Sir J. J. Inglis, *The Sepoy Revolt*, 1895
Lt.-Gen. Sir J. J. Inglis, *Lucknow and Oudh in the Mutiny*, 1895
Mrs. Muter, *My Recollections of the Sepoy Revolt*, 1897
Lady Inglis, *The Siege of Lucknow*, 1892
Mrs. J. P. Harris, *A Lady's Diary of the Siege of Lucknow*, 1858
R. G. Wilberforce, *An Unrecorded Chapter of the Indian Mutiny*, 1894

Regimental Names

5th Foot: THE NORTHUMBERLAND FUSILIERS
10th Foot: THE LINCOLNSHIRE REGIMENT
13th Foot: THE SOMERSETSHIRE LIGHT INFANTRY
16th Foot: THE BEDFORDSHIRE REGIMENT
37th Foot: THE HAMPSHIRE REGIMENT
39th Foot: THE DORSETSHIRE REGIMENT
44th Foot: THE ESSEX REGIMENT
53rd Foot: THE SHROPSHIRE LIGHT INFANTRY
60th Foot: THE KING'S ROYAL RIFLE CORPS
64th Foot: THE NORTH STAFFORDSHIRE REGIMENT
75th Foot: THE GORDON HIGHLANDERS
78th Foot: THE SEAFORTH HIGHLANDERS
84th Foot: THE YORK AND LANCASTER REGIMENT
95th Foot: THE RIFLE BRIGADE

Index

Afghanistan, 30, 32, 33, 36
Agra, 28, 65, 92, 136, 155
Akbar Khan, 52, 55, 56, 59, 60, 63
Alexander and Co., 28
Allahabad, 105, 106, 108, 109, 111–13, 119, 141, 155, 162–4
Ambala, 98
Amherst, Lord, 17
Anson, General, 89, 92, 97, 98, 165
Aong, 124, 165
Arakan, 17
Assam, 17
Auckland, Lord, 32, 33, 35, 36, 41, 46–8, 50
Ava, 20, 23
Ava, King of, 17, 18, 23
Avitabile, General, 67
Ayrton, Lieutenant, 118

Baird Smith, 103
Banks, Major, 148
Barnard, Sir Harry, 103
Barrackpore, 95
Barrackpore Park, 29
Barrett, 22
Barrow, Captain, 130, 132, 167
Beatson, Captain Stuart, 113, 133
Benares, 105, 106, 108, 111, 162
Bengal Native Infantry. *See* Infantry Regiments, 38th
Bentinck, Lady, 29
Bentinck, Lord Henry, 29
Birch, Colonel, 72
Bird, Wilberforce, 64
Bithur, 90, 104, 134, 141, 157, 159
Bithur, Peishwas of, 80, 110; *see also* Nana Sahib
Bombay, 14, 77, 89, 107
Bonn, 78
Bontein, Major, 94
Braxjun, 96
Brayser, Captain, 108, 112, 118, 167
Broadfoot, George, 38, 42, 46, 51–4, 58–60, 62, 63, 67, 68
Broadfoot, Captain William, 52
Brydon, Dr., 56, 57
Buffs (East Kent Regiment), 17
Bunni, 168
Burhampore, 95, 97
Burnes, Captain, 32–3, 36, 45, 52
Busherat-Gange, 152, 157, 165, 168
Bushire, 91, 92, 94, 96

Cachar, 17
Calcutta, 15, 22, 26, 35, 47, 74, 89, 106, 107, 162
Campbell, Sir Archibald, 18–21
Campbell, Sir Colin, 82, 111, 147, 159, 160, 162, 163, 165, 181, 182
Canning, Lord, 90, 91, 95, 96, 98, 103, 107, 108
Carabineers, 100, 101
Cawnpore, 24, 28, 65, 103–12, 114, 115, 121–8, 131–49, 153, 154, 156, 158, 160, 162, 163, 165, 166
Chamberlain, 103
Charterhouse, 10–12
Chillianwalia, 73
Chinhut, 148
Chinsura, 26, 28
Chitty, 12

Colville, 23
Combermere, 30
Cooper, Major, 167
Cotton, Sir Willoughby, 17, 24, 26, 31, 35, 37, 38, 47, 48, 70, 74
Crimean War, 90
Crommelin, 144, 157, 158, 166–8
Cureton, Colonel, 87
Curtis, Mrs., 66

Dada Sahib, 64
Dalhousie, Lord, 80, 83–6, 89, 90
Dartford, Kent, 9
Delhi, 84, 94, 97–100, 103, 106, 111, 136, 166, 173
Dinapore, 28, 147, 156, 160, 162, 164
Dost Mohammed, 32, 33, 36, 41, 43, 45
Dragoons, 3rd, 68
Dragoons, 4th, 14, 23
Dragoons, Light, 14th, 72
Dresden, 78
drunkenness, 15–16, 18–19, 139–40
Dum-Dum, 81, 94
Duncan, General, 38
Durand, Sir Henry, 35–6

East India Company, 75–7, 80, 85, 90, 107
Edwardes, Herbert, 36, 53
Ellenborough, Lady, 65
Ellenborough, Lord, 62, 64–7
Elphinstone, Lord, 97
Elphinstone, General, 22, 50–3, 55–8
Enam Commission, 80
Enfield rifle, 80–81, 94, 106, 112, 118–20, 124, 128, 131
Erin, 98
Eyre, 167, 172

Fane, Sir Henry, 30, 35–40, 47
Farrukhabad, 163
Fatehpur, 105, 117, 120, 123
'Feroze', 68
Ferozepore, 50, 54, 97
Ferozeshah, 68
Field Artillery, 100
Foot Regiments
  10th, 77, 86, 113, 146, 147
  13th, 13–17, 20, 22, 29, 30, 45, 51, 61, 89
  16th, 28
  35th, 51
  37th, 146, 147
  38th, 17
  53rd, 72, 74
  64th, 97, 112, 118, 122, 126, 130, 131, 133, 134, 153, 167, 180
  75th, 88
  84th, 112, 118, 130, 131, 156, 167, 176
  95th, 12, 13
Forbes, A., 156, 181
Fort William, 15, 24
Fortescue, *History of the British Army*, 37
Fusiliers, 5th, 147, 162, 163, 167, 175
Futtehabad, 54

Gardner, Lieutenant James, 14, 15, 22
General Kyd, 14
General Service Order, 90
Ghazni, 44–7
Gillespie, 101
Gough, Sir Hugh, 62, 64–8, 72–5, 118
Gough, Lady, 66
Gough, Miss, 66
Govindur, 82, 83
Graham, Brigadier, 38
Grant, Hope, 182
Grant, Sir Patrick, 98, 103, 111, 115, 140–4, 149, 156, 157, 160, 162
Grey, General, 65
Gubbins, M. R., 180, 182
Gujerat, 74, 75
Gundamuk, 52, 54
Gwalior campaign, 64–6

Hamilton, Colonel, 118, 167, 172, 182
Hardinge, Lord, 67, 70, 72, 75, 76, 86, 87, 89

Hargood, Lieutenant, 182
Havelock, Charles, 14
Havelock, Ettrick, 27
Havelock, Hannah, 24, 26–9, 71, 78–9, 89, 120, 138, 181
Havelock, Henry:
birth, 9; education, 9–12
Ensign in 95th Foot, 12; joins army of Burma, 18–19; in action in Burma, 20–22; rejoins army of Burma, 23; decorated by King of Ava, 23; history of the war in Burma, 11, 24–6; meets Hannah Marshman, 24; posts as interpreter, 24, 28, 47, 62; adjutancy of depot at Chinsura, 26; married, 26; attempt to purchase captaincy, 28, 30; adjutancy of 13th Foot, 29–30; A.D.C. to Cotton, 31; meets Ranjit Singh, 33; Afghanistan campaign, 37, 39–40, 41–5, 50–61; history of Afghan campaign, 38, 47–9, 62; Deputy Adjutant-General, 63; commands division in Kohistan, 63; Order of the Bath, 63; Major, 64; lieutenant-colonel by brevet, 66; Sikh war, 67–9; changes to 39th Foot, 70; becomes Deputy Adjutant-General, 70, 74–5; changes to 53rd Foot, 72; takes leave in Europe, 75–8; fails to buy lieutenant-colonelcy, 77; returns to India, 83; Quartermaster-General, 86–8; Adjutant-General, 89; colonel, 89; commands division in Persian war, 92, 94, 96–7; returns to India at outbreak of Mutiny, 97–8; command of column at Allahabad, 108–12; recapture of Cawnpore, 113–41; battle of Fatehpur, 117–20; advance on Cawnpore, 121–8; preparations to relieve Lucknow, 141–4; begins march on Lucknow, 144–51; replaced by Outram, 149, 160–1; actions at Busherat-Gange, 152–4, 157; criticised by Neill, 154–6; retires to Cawnpore, 159; awaits reinforcement of Cawnpore, 162–7; preparations for relief of Lucknow, 164, 167; advance to Lucknow, 167–9; battle of the Alum Bagh, 169–73; capture of Lucknow, 173–9; command of brigade at Lucknow, 180; K.C.B., baronet, 181; death, 181–2
family life, 27, 62, 64, 71, 75, 78; health, 22, 70–72, 75, 78, 142; love of the classics, 10–11, 13, 25; religious life, 9, 11, 14, 15, 20, 28, 29; views on drink, 15–16, 27, 29, 33, 41, 45, 123
Havelock, Henry (son), 27, 30, 71, 77, 86, 113, 133, 134, 138, 139, 144, 157–8, 176, 181, 182
Havelock, Joshua, 30, 71, 75–7
Havelock, Mrs. (mother), 9–11, 28
Havelock, William, 9, 11, 12, 14, 23, 25–6, 72–3
Havelock family, 9–12
Hearsey, General, 82, 95
Herat, 32, 33, 35, 36, 91
Hewitt, 101
Highlanders, 78th, 97, 112, 118, 122, 126, 130, 131, 133, 153, 162, 167, 172, 176, 177, 182
Horse Artillery, 44, 100
Hunter, Sir William, 113
Hyder Kahn, Mohammed, 44–5

Infantry Regiments:
6th (Native), 108
11th (Native), 99
19th (Native), 95, 96
20th (Native), 99
34th (Native), 95

Infantry Regiments—*continued*
35th (Native), 51
38th (Bengal Native), 83
42nd (Native), 156, 157, 159
47th (Native), 96
56th (Native), 118
66th (Native), 82
See also Buffs, Foot Regiments, Highlanders, Madras Infantry
Inglis, Sir J. J., 148, 164, 165, 174, 179, 180
Innes, Colonel McLeod, 147, 158
Inveraith, Lieutenant, 44

Jalalabad, 47, 52, 54–7, 59–62
Johnson, Lieutenant, 166, 168

Kabul, 32, 35, 36, 43, 45, 47, 50–53, 55, 56, 62, 63
Kalat, Kahn of, 42
Kandahar, 35, 43, 44, 47
Kashmir, 33
Keane, Sir John, 35, 41, 43–8
Kemmendine, 21
Kharak, 91
Khord Kabul Pass, 51, 56, 57, 63
Koh-i-noor diamond, 33, 46
Kurnaul, 16, 27, 28, 38
Kush-Ab, 96

Lahore, 48, 67, 68
Lancers, 9th, 166
Lancers, 16th, 14, 44
Landour, 27
Lawrence, Henry, 80, 103, 105, 106, 115, 137, 138, 147, 148
Leipsic, 77
Lloyd, General, 146
Lucknow, 103, 105–12, 115, 136–8, 141–4, 147–50, 155–8, 160, 164–9, 171, 173–82
Lugard, Colonel, 87

McGaskill, 63
MacGregor, Captain, 52, 58, 59
Mack, Dr., 28, 30–31
Mackintosh and Co., 28
Macnaghten, Sir William, 35–8, 46, 50, 51, 55
Madras, 47, 107
Madras Fusiliers, 107, 112, 115, 118, 124–6, 128, 130, 131, 140, 141, 153, 159, 162, 167, 176, 182
Madras Infantry, 164
Maharajpore, 65, 127
Manipur, 17
Mansfield, Major, 77
Markham, Colonel, 87, 89
Marshman, Hannah Shepherd. *See* Havelock, Hannah
Marshman, John Clark: *Havelock*, 9–10, 12; 24, 25, 28, 30, 48, 71, 87, 138, 176
Maude, F. C., 107–8, 112, 113, 117, 118, 123–5, 131, 133, 153, 159, 167, 172, 175–7
Meerut, 84, 97, 99–103
Military Club, 88
Minto, Lord, 32
Mohumbra, 97
Moira, Lord, 17
Monk Wearmouth, 9
Monteith, Colonel, 51, 53, 55, 59, 60
Mooltan Horse, 103
Moorsom, 178
Mudki, 67, 68
Muhesir, 42
Mungulwar, 152, 154, 158, 168

Nana Sahib, 80, 90, 103–5, 108–10, 115, 122, 126, 127, 131, 132, 134, 138, 141
Napadee, 23
Napier, Colonel, 149, 180
Napier, Sir Charles, 82, 83, 85
Napoleon, 11, 118, 119
Native Cavalry, 1st, 82
Native Cavalry, 2nd, 127
Native Cavalry, 3rd, 99

Native Infantry. *See* Infantry Regiments
Neill, Colonel James, 107–15, 122, 123, 141, 142, 144–7, 154–7, 166–7, 172, 175–8
Nicholls, Sir Jasper, 47, 62
Nicholson, John, 103

Oldfield, 51, 53, 54, 56, 59, 60
Olphert, Jack, 155, 159, 167, 172, 178
Onao, 153
Oudh, 80, 89, 94, 105
Outram, Sir James, 45, 80, 92, 96, 97, 107, 149, 160, 162, 165–7, 177–82

Paget, Sir Edward, 17, 96
Pandi, Mangal, 95
Patanago, 23
Pearson, Dick, 124, 182
Persia, 32, 33, 36, 91, 92, 96, 97, 107, 112, 167
Peshawar, 33, 47, 54, 55, 57–60, 82
Pollock, General, 57, 59–62
Poona, 23
Pottinger, Major, 63
Prome, 23
Punjab, 35, 80
Punniar, 65

Queen's Regiment, 84th, 95

Raine, Dr., 10
Ramnuggur, 72, 87
Ramsay, General, 47
Ramsay, Lieutenant-Colonel Balcarres, 88
Rangoon, 17–19, 22
Ranjit Singh, 33, 35, 36, 38, 39, 46, 67
Rawalpindi, 82
Renaud, Major, 109, 112, 113, 115, 116, 118, 124, 137
Rifles, 60th, 100, 101
Rifles, 90th, 147, 162, 163, 167, 172
Roberts, Lord, 103
Russia, 32, 33, 91

Sale, Sir Robert, 14, 15, 29, 30, 44, 45, 51–5, 57–60, 62, 67, 68, 88
Schwallbach Springs, 76
Seaton, Sir T., 42
Sepoys, 81–5, 90, 93–6, 100, 108, 112, 118, 124–7, 129–32, 134, 146, 153, 158, 159, 168, 171, 172
Serampore, 24, 26
Shah Sujah-ul-Mulk, 33, 35, 36, 41–7, 50–52, 58–60
Shahpuri, 17
Shekhabad, 45
Sherer, J. W., 120, 137, 138
Shorncliffe, 12, 13
Sikh war, 67–9
Sikhs, 108, 112, 116, 118, 122–3, 130, 131, 140, 167, 176, 180
Simla, 64
Sind, 35, 36, 80
Smith, General Harry, 63, 64, 68–9
Smith, Mrs. Harry, 66
Snodgrass, Major J. J., 19
Sobraon, 69
Somerset, Sir Henry, 98
Spiers, Colonel, 64
Stalker, General, 92
Stephenson, Major, 126
Stirling, Major, 118, 133

Tezin, 63
Topee, Tantia, 66, 110, 126–9
Trevelyan, G. M., 104
Tucker, Robert Clare, 120, 102
Tucker, Colonel, 81
Tytler, Lieutenant-Colonel Fraser, 113, 116, 117, 124, 144, 157, 158, 164, 169, 176

United Service Club, 75

van Alten, General, 12
Vellore, 101
Vicovich, Count, 32–3
Victoria, Queen, 75
Vienna, 78

Waterloo, 76
Wazirabad, 82
Wellington, Duke of, 12, 18, 19, 70, 75, 76, 160
Wheeler, Sir Hugh, 103–6, 108, 109, 139
Wilde, Colonel, 57
Willis, 176
Willmer, Lieutenant, 44
Willoughby, 103
Wilson, Archdale, Brigadier, 101
Wright, Captain, 94

Yandaboo, 23